W9-DDP-535

MANDALAS

for Power & Energy

Marion and Werner Küstenmacher

STERLING PUBLISHING CO., INC.
New York

Published by Sterling Publishing Co., Inc.
387 Park Avenue South, New York, N.Y. 10016
Originally published in Germany under the title
Energie und Kraft durch Mandalas © 1998 by W. Ludwig Buchverlag
in the Sudwest Verlag GmbH & Co. KG, Munich.
English Translation © 2003 by Sterling Publishing Co., Inc.
Distributed in Canada by Sterling Publishing
^c/_o Canadian Manda Group, One Atlantic Avenue, Suite 105
Toronto, Ontario, Canada M6K 3E7
Distributed in Great Britain by Chrysalis Books
64 Brewery Road, London N7 9NT, England
Distributed in Australia by Capricorn Link (Australia) Pty. Ltd.
P.O. Box 704, Windsor, NSW 2756 Australia

Printed in China
All rights reserved

Sterling ISBN 1-4027-0546-8

Contents

Preface

This book about Mandalas is a kind of Mandala in itself. It is the result of an exciting inner journey that has led us through stacks of art volumes and vast collections of ornaments; we could never tell when this journey was going to come to an end. Like the never-ending roundness of the Mandala, we have been circling, together with the artists of different epochs and cultures, around a sometimes invisible but always perceivable center.

Many people have colored our re-imaginings of old ornaments and have given us encouragement and advice. We would like to express our gratitude to all of them and hope that their expertise will be helpful to the users of this book.

We would like to invite you to join us on this journey, to take your place in the long line of people who have designed Mandalas and created with their own colors ever new variations.

Marion and Werner Küstenmacher

Introduction

What is a Mandala?

The word "Mandala" originated in the classical Indian cultural language of Sanskrit and simply means "circle." Though the unfamiliar word comes from a far-off country, the depiction of it is found in all religions and cultures as a circle, wheel, wreath, rotation, circulation, round dance or just simply—dancing.

Circle and Center

The mathematical definition of the circle is also simple: a number of points that all are the same distance from a center. The circle is defined by its center; it exists solely because of it—however, this center does not have to be visible at all, for, as a mathematical point, it has, strictly speaking, no necessary visible expansion. Each circular form, each plate, each coin has a center that is only in the rarest cases indicated or seen directly. And yet we can feel that center, can imagine it, and make it visible before our spiritual eye.

Thus, the circle becomes a distinctly religious symbol. The center is the equivalent of God, the One, the origin, the mysterious, the metaphysical, the center behind all visible nature. Our world, moreover, takes place on the circle; it is defined by its distance from the origin. Our life gains its inner form through the center point around which it turns.

Reconciliation of Extremes

A circle is dynamic. "The number of points" can actually be thought of only in the circle's movement, just as the compass moves across the paper or as the beam of light from a lighthouse writes its fading line on land and sea. The vital swing of the circle is only possible through the stable lasting nature of its center. They need each other—point and circle, silence and dance, content and form, God and world, one and many, as well as seeds and fruit. Thus, the circle becomes the mirror reflection of the all-encompassing. It is the most profound symbol for the secret of life that is constantly drawn back and forth between extremes: on the one hand, the complete here and now, the drowning in matter and form, and, on the other hand, the escape from this world, the idealistic path through meditation and ecstasy.

Ottoman rose window
in the dome of the mosque of Sultan Soliman I,
Constantinople, Turkey (beginning of the 16th century)

Celtic spiral, from the *Book of Kells*,
Trinity College Library, Dublin, Ireland (9th century)

Rosette in the apses of the Cathedral of Mailand (15th century)

The Circle in Religion

Each religion has tried to find formulas for the reconciliation of opposites, pictures for bringing together the center and the circumference—God and world. The Christian mystic Meister Eckhart intimates, so to speak, the creed of the circle when he says: "God is inside, we are outside." "Pray and work," thus becomes the advice for the centering of life's energy, according to the founder of the Benedictines of Nursia.

The Sufi master Ibn Arabi formulates it this way: "Were God to be separated from the world for only one blink of an eye, the world would vanish at the very same moment. However, the light that radiates from His appearance is so mighty that we cannot perceive it, but only recognize His creation—which conceals Him at the same time."

The inner goal of our life is to find the center. Not that we could ever reach it and subsequently "have" it, but the form of our life permits us to surmise the existence of the center. If we could not do that, our life would no longer make sense. We would feel at odds with ourselves, split, stressed, and ill at ease with our own being. From Hermann Hesse comes the exclamation: "Having one's home in oneself! How different life would be! It would have a center and from its center all power could radiate. My life, however, does not have a center, but hovers twitchingly between many rows and poles and counter-poles."

7

The Closed Garden

Therefore, each way of looking for the center of life—for the real goal of life—is in fact a search for our own personal center. It is always there within us; it cannot be lost. Inseparably connected with the divine, it is also hidden, forgotten, and at times missed. The secret that "I am" and the secret that "God is" are in the end one and the same. Coming closer to this secret is a basic instinct of the human being. It is the search for the lost paradise, the closed garden that holds everything, a place in which we are perfectly happy, and in which all our needs are satisfied. An important feature of each Mandala is the outer border, so to speak, the wall around the closed garden.

Our life often suffers from the anxiety of unclear borders. How many tasks do we have to be occupied by? Constantly increasing media and new means of communication present us with more and more unsolvable questions, and bring the needs of an entire world into our house every day. In earlier times, children were allowed to limit themselves to their small naïve world; today, however, they also know more and more and are likewise confronted with overwhelming connections to a society that is becoming ever more strongly networked.

The Mandala provides a salutary limitation. It is a clear and marked-off area. The task of filling it with colors is easy to grasp. The figure of the Mandala is concentrated on one center point, and the small garden invites us to spend time there and to disclose its complexities in studied observation.

The Circle—The Beginning of Culture

The representation of the circle marks the beginning of human culture. Circular structures appear among the oldest restored buildings of humankind—the mysterious stone circle of Stonehenge, for example, and the giant Neolithic round castles in Ireland. With the wheel and a potter's wheel, crafts and science begin. With the exploration of the cyclical repetitions of seasons and periods of fertility, a productive and systematically planned agriculture develops.

One of the oldest Mandalas is the sun disk, the model of all circular figures, giver of all life. Often it is run through by curved lines—put into motion and limited by rays or small triangles. The circle of the sun, symbol of force and movement, is itself in motion: it rises, wanders across the sky, and sets once again.

Sumerian Seal with cross-shaped motif, Susa (about 4000 B.C.E.)

The conscious and expressed experience of returning, the regular alteration of sunlight and darkness, of day and night, of high tide and low tide, the sequence of the moon's phases—all these mark an important early stage in the development of humankind.

The Mandala and the Cross

Though fascinated by the symbol of the dynamic circle, we need to remember that there are other important realizations in the continuing maturation of the human spirit. One of them is the awareness of the nonrepetitive quality of time, the painful truth that our life has a beginning and an end, and that our possibilities are limited. All old religions imagine God as someone who is remote from this up and down reality of experience. Jewish belief dared a revolution in its thinking when it posited a God who has an effect on the life of man, directly interfering at very specific times—a God who can be experienced without abolishing the limitless distance between God and the world.

Circular thinking retreats in Judaism. Not the eternal return, but the uniqueness of our earthly action steps into the foreground. This dynamic comes to completion in the Christian ideal of the incarnation of God. God takes on human appearance at a very certain point of time in history and at a very certain place. Center and diameter meet through the cross. The model of the cross is the coming together of two lines that lose themselves in the infinite.

The Christian monks found a tangible equivalent for the combination of Incarnation and Infinity when they did missionary work among the Celts in today's Ireland. Here they succeeded in fusing the

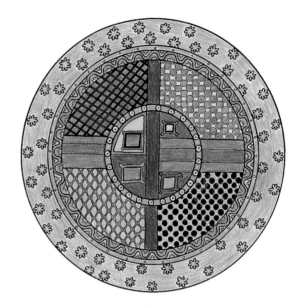

"The Fixed Star Sphere," detail of a miniature, France (14th century)

Celtic heritage with the New Testament. The most impressive proof is the Celtic Cross in which both symbols entwine. The circle, which is divided four times, is reminiscent of the compass that indicates the four cardinal points. From its small circle, the infinity of the sky can be represented and studied. On the other hand, the Mandala that is divided into four parts can be experienced as a "compass towards the inside," a means for inner orientation.

Mandala and the Symbolism of Numbers

Beside the number four, many other numbers appear in Mandalas. How often certain pictorial elements are repeated is often connected with the conscious or unconscious symbolism of the number.

Numbers have always had more than an abstract and quantitative meaning—the meanings we ascribe to them today. Each number also has a very certain quality and vivid symbolism that flows into the Mandala. Numbers open up relationships, establish connections, arrange, and interpret. They therefore become the key to reality and its mysteries. Surprisingly, the interpretative patterns are similar for very different societies, so at this point we'd like to provide a few key words for the numbers one through nine.

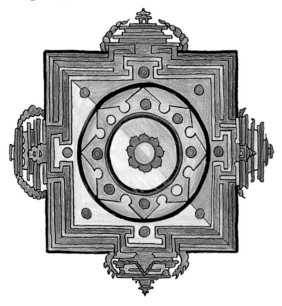

Tibetan mandala in the form of a heavenly palace (19th century)

One: Beginning, core, origin, unity, uniqueness, earnestness, centralization, the unique and timeless, the undivided and unifying, expression of the highest idea, attribute, and nature of God.

Two: The feminine, encounter, unification, pair, belonging together and intimacy, polarity, tension, differentiation, doubt, disagreement, discord, ambivalence, rupture, opposition, division, separation.

Three: The masculine, life, movement, impetus, energy, development, creative spirit, fertility, fulfillment, completeness (man, woman, and child; beginning, middle, and end; body, spirit, and soul, etc.), completeness, trinity.

Four: The earthly, four elements, cardinal points and seasons, the four functions of consciousness (thinking, feeling, sensing, intuition), order, firmness, structure, stability, quietness, balance, sacred wedding.

Five: Encounter, unification, number of Venus, centralized wholeness, five Chinese elements (earth, water, fire, wood, metal), five basic pillars of Islamic belief (proclamation of faith, prayer, fasting, alms, pilgrimage), cosmos, health, salvation, transcendence, quintessence, fullness, completion.

Six: Heaven and earth, God and man, female and male, unification of opposites, satisfaction.

Seven: Renewal of the human organism, hope, refreshing, stimulation, comfort, seven days, seven decades of life, seven sacraments, seven virtues, arts and sciences, entity, fullness.

Eight: Quietness, harmony, realization, perfection, rising, resurrection, confidence, salvation, eight-fold path of Buddha.

Nine: Transformation, new birth, nine museums, nine angel choruses (Judaism), nine heavenly spheres (China), nine worlds (Germanic myth).

Mandala and Contemplation

Especially in Buddhism, Mandalas play an important role as a means for religious contemplation. The Mandalas of the Tibetan monks are famous: giant figures made out of colored sand that are spread out on the ground of the monastery, representing weeks of work. As soon as the Mandala is completed, though, it will be destroyed. It is not about a completed piece of art, but about the process of its production. The path itself is the goal. That the term "Mandala" has become famous we owe above all to the psychoanalytic thinker C. G. Jung. He himself had experienced how Mandalas can work inside of us as "magnets" for contradictory mental material. In painted or colored Mandalas, he claimed, structures of the soul are expressed "that surpass the individual and are brought into the encompassing rhythm of cosmic life." People can detect in the symbol of the Mandala, independent of its origin and culture, that they do not have to become lost on the path of existence but can rather find security in a center.

Mandala and the Labyrinth

We can find a typical western form of the Mandala in the labyrinth. The "classical" labyrinth is not the maze with its multiple forks, but the closed winding path. Should we walk it, we would be forced into multiple outer paths in order to travel around our proper center. Only when we have cut off the interior completely and experienced all the dimensions of our being, can we reach the center. Many medieval cathedrals had a labyrinth mosaic situated in the ground in the vicinity of the entrance, around which a special liturgical dance was performed at the Easter service.

The path to completion consists of fate-determined detours and wrong tracks. It is, according to Jung, "a very long street"—not a straight stretch but a wavy line that links opposites: "a path whose labyrinthine intertwining does not lack horror." In this way, experiences come about that are often called "difficult to access." Their inaccessibility is based on the fact that they are costly: they demand that we confront that which we fear most. And they traffic in the wholeness that we continuously carry in our mouth and with which we can theorize eternally, yet give a wide berth in real life. C.G. Jung has called this path of life "individuation," which leads like the winding paths of the labyrinth to one's true center: the not-yet-manifested "whole" human being that is the greater and future one.

Floor labyrinth in the Cathedral of St. Quentin, France

It is probably no coincidence that the maze has driven out the "one-way labyrinth" in the past two centuries. It marks the desire of the human being to make decisions himself.

Coloring

"Coloring" is much more than simply working at a piece of paper with crayons. It is a ritual, a dance around the center, carried out by pencils that leave their color marks. When we color, we "set off." We follows each individual line of the drawing. We become engrossed and retreat into the boundaries of the picture; at the same time, however, we also open up that which we, and only we, can find there. We have our own magic with which to follow the lines of an artist who designed them precisely many centuries ago.

Detail of a new-Gothic glass window in St. Thomas, Strasbourg, France (around 1860)

The Vivid Line

Thus, you will not find any models in this book that have been created by a computer or other technical drawing equipment. Except for some circles that have been drawn with a thick felt pen in a circle, all lines have been drawn by hand. The naturalness and vividness of the human, slightly imperfect structure keep the coloring from melting together with the shape.

As we color, we only seem to walk on predrawn paths. Actually, we are creating the paths anew, choosing colors systematically or quite spontaneously—color shades of our heart or colorful lights of our inspiration. The crayon, the chalk, the brush—they turn white paper, limited by thin black lines, into spaces. They give the space structure and invigorate it with pencil lines or blurry traces of the brush.

Because the Mandala is already complete, it does not demand perfection. It does not need or even want any perfection—even though confronting our own need for perfection can certainly be an experience with the coloring of Mandalas. Even a partly colored, "incomplete" Mandala is valid—sometimes even that which we can "give up"—that part of the Mandala that we leave white—radiates an even greater depth of knowledge concerning ourselves and our strengths.

When you color, you receive a share in the creative principle of our world. The virtually unlimited variety of forms is multiplied by a variety of possible color combinations that seems unlimited as well. If you design the same motif at different times or have it colored by different people, you may be surprised about the differences and richness of the results.

Coloring in Silence

Silence is inherent in the coloring of Mandalas and comes about automatically. This is the wonderful experience many teachers talk about—that takes place when children color Mandalas: they gradually become quiet and concentrate on their picture.

Silence helps us find our way toward the inside. The search for the center to which the Mandala invites us is the search for our personal home country, our completeness, the reconciliation of opposites, the abolition of polarity. Strength and energy wait in this inner center for us, as do equanimity, calm, and composure.

Limitless Figures

The most important rule when coloring a Mandala is that there are no rules! You may start either from the outside and work toward the inside, or begin in the center, or you may feel your way in a clockwise or counter-clockwise direction; or you may begin randomly at several spots or according to an inner system—there are many approaches and ways to experience the secret of the circle and center. You are not obliged to fill all the white areas of the paper with color. Some people who have had several years of experience with it, report on the increasing transparency of their Mandalas. They leave a great deal open and feel less and less the urge to color in all the pre-drawn forms.

Coloring with Children

We can draw some interesting conclusions from the way children proceed in coloring Mandalas, espe-cially when they tackle them before they have worked with other inner/outer systems. Those who have a strong inner center usually start in the middle. Thus, children who appear nervous and insecure may reveal that they are stable on the inside and have a healthy basic trust in their parents. Likewise, introverted children will prefer the movement from the inside to the outside: they slowly conquer the outside world starting from their inner center.

Children who are very strongly searching for the sense and goal of their life will tend to work from the edge towards the center. The more systematically they proceed, the further they have developed in their inner process. Extroverted children also seem to prefer starting from the outside. However, be careful not to overinterpret or evaluate: any one coloring style is as good as another.

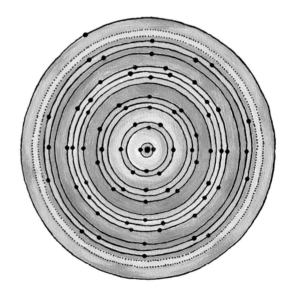

Flat representation of gold (element 79)

Which of the Mandalas in our collection are best suited for children? You will find a list of them at the back of this book. Nevertheless, do not underestimate children. They are quite capable of coloring Mandalas all by themselves, without help. Complicated patterns may fascinate them and increase their concentration. Try not to judge, even if the children leave their Mandalas incomplete. This might be due more to the complicated pattern than to the impatience of the children. Some motifs in this book are deliberately elaborate so that even people with advanced skills find fun and challenge in coloring them. But from age 10 on up, children can work on all the motifs.

About the Texts in this Book

On the left-hand page of each Mandala motif, you will find a title that is a kind of mnemonic device. It is not necessarily the correct cultural or historical designation, but it is meant to stimulate your curiosity and make it easier to find things.

Below the title is a meditative text which, in most cases, comes from the same cultural circle as the picture. Sometimes this text creates an interesting contrast—let yourself be surprised. It is often followed by some short enlightening sentences about the cultural-historical and symbolic background of the motif.

At the bottom of the page, you will find its designation, the place where it was discovered and the age of the original Mandala design. We could not always determine precise information, since we always selected the most beautiful, vigorous, and energetic motifs, even if their origin could not be established incontestably.

We have also provided coloring tips for many

Sun wheel, carved motif on a stone stele from Gotland, Sweden (most likely 6th century)

motifs, some small assists and ideas for meditation and concentration as you work on each figure. Please take them as an incentive and as something you can do if you choose, but not as a task or anything you must do.

When you take up colored pencils, felt pens, crayons, or a brush, and become engrossed in these often ancient shapes and patterns, you don't have to worry about right or wrong, about rules or recommendations, but only about one thing—becoming free, freeing yourself from your surroundings, or even better—forgetting them entirely and gaining energy and power by doing so.

MANDALAS
for Coloring

You will get the most beautiful results if you place a thin piece of cardboard under the Mandala you are coloring. Colored pencils, crayons, or felt pens will work best. Water colors are not recommended.

Man in the Labyrinth

*There is only one path in this world in
which nobody can go except yourself.
Do not ask where it leads! Follow it!*

Friedrich Nietzsche

Among the Naskapi Indians, the aborigines of the Labrador islands, there exists the idea of a
companion inside the soul, whom they call "My Friend" or "Great Man." They believe he lives in
the heart of each one of them and speaks to them through dreams. Whoever follows his instruc-
tions receives from him a complete sense of orientation: whether hunting in the wilderness, or
performing tribal customs, or experiencing close relationships—the "Great Man" inside shows
everyone the way.

Follow your "inner friend" with colors through this labyrinth, completely led by your intuition.

"Man in the Labyrinth," motif on wickerwork, Native American tradition, Arizona, U.S.A.
(20th century)   ➤

Chinese Flower

I have noticed that, on a tree, there is always a sprout of a future flower already hidden behind the wilting leaf. Thus, also, life in the young, fresh, and vigorous body is the nourishing cover of the spiritual flower. As it wilts and falls off in its earthly time, the spirit arises from it as an eternal heavenly flower.

Bettina von Arnim, writer (1785–1859)

This Chinese Mandala not only contains a flower in its center, as you can perceive when you observe it closely, but it also has fruits on the outside, shooting out between the narrow leaves. Thus, it does not only embody growth, but also the concurrence of nonconcurrence. It abolishes our idea of time, in which events take place one after the other. It combines what is separated by time, but is essentially one: each fruit is a transformed flower.

Let this Mandala grow from the inside to the outside, and delight in each step from the center of the flower up to the ripe fruit.

Floral detail of a Chinese picture, according to an illustration in an English art guide
(19th century)   ➤

The Grecian Eight

For each soul, the circular movement means penetration from the outside to the proper depth. Thus, a concentration of spiritual forces protect it from deviations and lead it back to the center, away from the multitude of outer things. In this way, it can compose itself in the heart of the soul—at the bottom of the soul.

Dionysius the Areopagite, philosopher (around 150 C.E.)

In this Mandala, something arises from a horizontal eight, which we use as a sign for infinity. Called "Lemniskate" (double loop) by the Greeks, it expresses a hovering harmony—full of spirit with its swinging poles—which is awarded to the sacred. The unity of the great circle with the eight swinging circles in it elucidates the movement between the earthly and spiritual world.

When coloring we notice that a single band wraps around the center in eight whirls. Each of the eight inner rays aims at each one of these whirling points. These are all connections we may express with colors, if we wish.

The horizontal eight connects both halves of the brain and thus fosters concentration and receptivity.

Marble relief on the outer wall, Small Metropolis, Athens (6th to 8th century) ➤

Sign of the Stone Mason

And you are waiting, awaiting the one thing,
that increases your life infinitely;
the powerful, the enormous,
the awakening of the stones,
depths, turned towards you.

Rainer Maria Rilke, poet (1875–1926)

It is an ancient desire of the human being to work on stone and to leave his mark in stone. These signs can outlast our own life. The stone is our symbol for the unconscious core in man. It is not only children who collect stones from the roadside with great dedication; adults also bring home "special" stones as if they contained a reviving secret. The stone stands for that part inside of us that can no longer dissolve, that cannot become lost, and is therefore felt to be eternal.

This Mandala can either be colored or painted onto a flat stone or carved into a soft Ytong stone. Children may try to reproduce it with colored chalk on the sidewalk. They can also be asked to create their own "stone sign," which will be placed with many other small stones on the ground. Don't forget to take pictures!

Medieval sign of the stone mason ➤

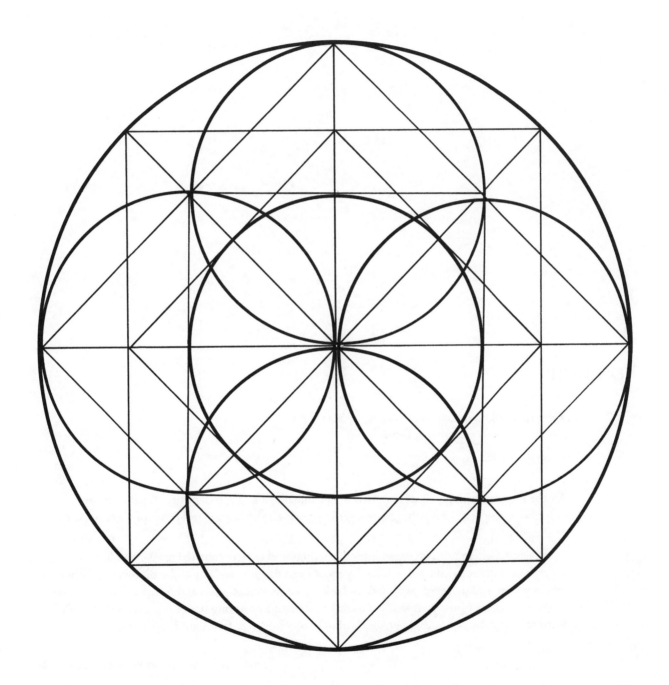

23

Pompeii

The first sign of mental composure is, in my opinion,
being able to pause and persevere within oneself.

Seneca, Roman philosopher (3 B.C.E.–65 C.E.)

All the mosaics in Pompeii were buried under thick layers of ash deposits. Yet the volcanic eruption in the year 79 C.E. has permanently preserved the beauty and color of these artistic ornaments.

Mandalas may help us to lay open buried offerings and buried knowledge. We can learn how much beauty there is under the dusty layers of everyday life, waiting to be discovered. When we take our time and persevere within ourselves, we come across good and fertile ground at some point: we discover how luxuriantly we are growing and flowering under our gray surface. We learn to enjoy the riches that our soul willingly sets free in extravagant beauty and abundance.

Antique floor mosaic in Pompeii, Italy ➤

Sun Wheel

First it is necessary to make the organ of sight correspond to and be similar to the object that is to be observed. Never could the eye have perceived the sun if it had not taken on the shape of the sun first; likewise the soul cannot recognize beauty until it has first become beautiful itself.

Plotinus, Greek philosopher (204–270 C.E.)

This eight-fold whirl with triangular rays stands for the all-invigorating sun. On the original, the single "shovels" of the whirl turn on a dark background. You can recreate this light-dark effect when coloring.

Light, shadow, and life are the themes of this Mandala, so that it is particularly suitable for children and "beginners" in Mandala coloring.

Sun Wheel, a chiseled motif on a stone stele from Gotland, Sweden (probably 6th century C.E.) ➤

Weave

The location of the soul is
where inner and outer worlds meet.
Where they penetrate,
it is in each point of the penetration.

Novalis, writer (1772–1801)

The Celtic weaves have manifold meanings. In pre-Christian times, an outsider was not allowed to enter the sacred Haynes without bonds; the weaves therefore expressed the devoted connection to the deity. In Christian times, the cross tied from the weaves stands for the Son of God, who lies in a "woven death shroud" and at last breaks all bonds.

Because the band ornaments of this Mandala are distinctly reminiscent of floral climbing plants, the inner shape of the cross may also be seen as a tree of life, through which shines the light of the sun surrounding it (the outer circle).

Book ornament in an optical weaving in a Celtic Sacramentary (book with liturgical texts),
Rheims, France ➤

Alhambra Star

The entire day I think about it
and speak it in the evening at last.
Where did I come from and what is expected of me?
I have no idea.
My soul derives from someplace else, of that I am sure,
and to end in that place is my goal.
…Yet who is this just now in my ear,
who perceives my voice?
Who speaks words with my mouth?
Who looks around with my eyes?
What is the soul?
…Whoever has brought me here,
will have to put me back.

Jalaluddin Rumi, Persian mystical poet (1207–1273)

Illustrations of God or people are forbidden in Islam—as in Judaism. Thus, Islamic art created geometric figures with inexhaustible fantasy. Glorious colors were added to the play of lines and patterns. Floors, walls, ceilings, carpets, or ceramic receptacles—everything was covered with the most delicate work of lines or luxuriant ornaments.

The art arising from the icon leaves much space for inner pictures. It depicts in a fascinating manner the inner patterns of our soul that are different from those pictures that are daily before our eyes.

Detail of a ceiling in the Moorish style in the entrance hall of the "Courtyard at the Fish Pond," Alhambra, Granada, Spain (14th century)　➤

The Inner Fortress

If one descends into oneself,
then what is found is precisely
what is desired.

Simone Weil, French philosopher (1909–1943)

Many people do not find the way to their inner being since they shy away from being alone or are afraid of loneliness. A certain degree of singleness or solitude, however, is necessary in order to be able to follow the path to the inside.

This Mandala is very well suited to ease this first step towards the inside. One wall after the other is to be overcome, from the outside to the inside or the other way around. A silent hour spent with coloring brings us back to ourselves. It discloses the well-protected spaces of our soul fortress. It opens the inner treasure chamber and helps distribute a whole wealth of personal energy that can be effective on very deep levels.

Geometrical structure for growing realization, Alchemist tradition (18th century) ➤

33

The Diamond

Each one of us possesses a divine spark; however, not everyone brings it to light as fully as possible. The spark is like a diamond; the latter cannot spread its radiance if it is hidden in the earth. But each one of us contains the light as from a diamond, as soon as we make it shine in the suitable setting.

Hasidic wisdom

Precious stones, and here particularly diamonds, are impressive symbols of the richness of the inner self. It is the greatest possible fortune for treasure hunters to find them and to see their inner light radiate—whether in the outer or inner world. A diamond needs light from the outside, which it can reflect a thousand times over in all colors of the rainbow. The right cutting and the suitable setting make it possible.

Look for the uncut diamond in your own labyrinth of life and make it shine through its proper setting. By the way, particularly expensive and big stones have a name. Find such a name for yourself as well—your soul is worth more than the most precious diamond.

Hedge labyrinth "The Diamond" in Russborough, England (1989) ➤

Star of the Quakers

Go placidly amid the noise and haste
and remember what peace there may be in silence.
As far as possible without surrender, be on good terms with all persons.
Speak your truth quietly and clearly and listen to others,
even the dull and ignorant; they too have their story.
Avoid loud and aggressive persons; they are vexatious to the spirit...

Be yourself.
Especially do not feign affection.
Neither be cynical about love,
for in the face of all aridity and disappointment
it is as perennial as the grass...

You are a child of the universe no less than the trees and the stars.
You have a right to be here.
And whether it is clear to you or not,
no doubt the universe is unfolding as it should.
Therefore be at peace with God,
whatever you conceive him to be,
and whatever your labors and aspirations in the noisy confusion of life,
keep peace with your soul...

From "Desiderata" —Old St. Paul's Church in Baltimore, Md.

The Quakers are a 300-year old protestant, pacifist community that has become native in the U.S.A. They are masters of silence. During their meetings, they remain silent most of the time, wishing to provide all kinds of space to the great secrets of life, without driving them away with a flood of words. The silent handcraft, in which wonderful quilts are sewn and stitched, is likewise part of the daily meditative program of Quaker women. It is in silence, they believe, that the presence of the divine can be experienced most distinctly. In silence we unfold most easily and achieve harmony with the universe.

"Star and Feathers" quilt in the Quaker style, U.S.A. (beginning of the 20th century)   ➤

Rose Window in the Cathedral of Magdeburg

Now, little human being, escape your occupation with the earthly for some time; hide a little bit from your noisy thoughts; throw away your troublesome worries and set aside your laborious distractions! Be a little bit there for God, rest in him for some time! Enter the chamber of your spirit and lock out everything besides God and that which helps you find Him! Look for him with a locked door.

Anselm of Canterbury, saint (1033–1109)

The most famous Gothic window rosettes are not windows through which you can look outside. They are "locked" to the outside through their colored glass and are, therefore, in the deepest sense, windows to the inside. You can first detect their actual beauty in the sacred room when the sun throws its light on them from the outside. The Mandala can create a similar situation: We turn our glance toward our inner being, supported by an outer structure that only serves to gradually reveal the colorful beauty that has awaited us, hidden on the inside.

This simple rosette opens, in many ways, windows to the inside. It is very appropriate for our first coloring experience with the wonderful world of Gothic rosettes.

Gothic Rose Window in the Cathedral of Magdeburg, Germany (around 1320) ➤

Growing from the Center

The great deeds of humankind are not those that make a lot of noise. Great things happen simply—like the trickling of water, the flowing of air, and the growing of grain.

Adalbert Stifter, poet (1805–1868)

Creation happens so naturally and silently that we seldom perceive it. It can be said that nature brings with it the "right attitude" and an infallible feeling for time: everything is allowed to grow in its own way and at the right time from the center. Nature does not allow itself to be pushed. On the other hand, it is not fixed either. It is not on the lookout for permanence, as we human beings are; it permits itself continuous change.

Flowing, streaming, growing, transfusing, ripening, dissolving, beginning anew—with this natural attitude we can enter into Mandala coloring and be surprised at what grows from its center.

Mandala, according to four colorfully glazed tiles, Central Europe (13th/14th century) ➤

Sun of Fire

Just as the one sun
illuminates the entire earth,
thus the divine self fills
the entire nature with light.
The magnificence that resides in the sun
and fulfills the entire world,
that is reflected in the moon and the fire,
recognizes the glory of God.

From the *Bhagavad Gita*, the holy book of India

The sun is probably the most important worldwide symbol for warmth, light, life, and whole-ness. With the sun disk, the human being expresses religious experiences as well. The individual attributes divine qualities to the sun or meditates upon it as a magnificent creation of God. As with any other round symbol, the sun bowl is also an allegory for the soul, whose inner light radiates outwards.

Let yourself be illuminated by the fiery light of this medieval Sun-Mandala.

Printer's mark (end of the 15th century) ➤

Bambara

A mentally balanced human being
is a human being
who has become conscious
of his blessings.

From Africa

Bambara is as cheerful as the bright light of the sunrise—a subject that can be found in innumerable variations in West African paintings. In a lively, almost merry manner, symmetry and imbalances mingle in these hand-painted patterns.

Children have an immediate affinity to such patterns and are easily encouraged to design individual Mandalas of this kind.

Traditional Bambara pattern printed on fabric, Mali, Africa ➤

The Circle of Limoges

The purpose of art is the search for beauty, as the purpose of religion is the search for God and truth. And just as art stops, thus also religion stops, when it stops looking for God and truth, believing to have found it.

Piotr Demianovitch Ouspensky, mathematician, author, teacher (1878–1947)

"Enamel," when translated, means "molten." With enamel techniques, multicolored, liquid glass masses are fused in such a way that new bright colors and effects of great beauty arise. All beauty, after all, is only waiting to be perceived—today, here, now. It wishes to penetrate into our innermost being. Beauty is the outer expression of a joy in union residing in the heart of the entire creation. Wherever it touches your center, it has a kind of triggering effect: it triggers an opening up and a desire for connection, a cosmic principle.

Try, with this Mandala, to have the colors overlap and run into each other. And enjoy yourself in your own ability for fusion.

Byzantine enamel décor, Limoges, France (end of the 12th century)　➤

Stonebreak

To see a world in a grain of sand
And a heaven in a wild flower,
Hold infinity in the palm of your hand
And eternity in an hour.

William Blake, poet, artist, and mystic (1757–1827)

Countless Mandalas can be found in the floral world. In the original photograph that served as a model for this Mandala, the foliage is only about an inch (2.5cm) in diameter. In the enlargement on the facing page, it is already symbolically "alienated," and if you color it with other shades beside the natural green, you will achieve further charming variations.

Stonebreak, according to a photograph of Karl Blossfeldt, (1929)   ➤

Three-Fold Spiral

Three folds the priest's robe has—
and yet it is woven from one piece.
Three joints has the finger—
and yet they move together.
Threefold is the clover—
and yet it is called the shamrock.
White frost, snow, and ice—
everything dissolves into water.
Three people are in God—
and yet he is always the same Holy One.

Irish folk saying

We can find the number three in multiple variations in this Mandala. Many Irish prayers and blessings contain hints about the Trinity, including the Irish flag with its threefold shamrock.

Discover as you color how the three areas engulf each other and become a single dancing unit.

Celtic spiral décor, *Book of Durrow*, Trinity College Library, Dublin (end of 7th century)   ➤

Star of David

I know that whatever God does endures forever;
nothing can be added to it, nor anything taken from it...
That which is, already has been;
That which is to be, already has been;
and God seeks what has been driven away.

Ecclesiastes 3.14–15

The six-pointed star, made from two equilateral triangles inserted into each other, can be found in many cultures. This example, which works in an additional circle, originated in Byzantine motifs.

Called the "Star of David," this figure is a relatively young tradition stemming from the Middle Ages. It has been a clear symbol of the Jewish religion since the 19th century. In 1897, it became the symbol for Zionism and, in 1948, with the founding of the state of Israel, the official emblem of the Jewish people as well.

When coloring you will notice how the perception oscillates between the triangles and the entire star, between the dynamic and the static.

After an ornament in St. Sebald, Nuremberg (15th century) ➤

Eight Leaves of Fortune

On the peak of the mountain
a flag is placed, one meter square.
Do not think the flag small!
On it, are eight leaves of fortune gathered.

On the peak of the mountain,
a pink flower grows.
Do not think the flower small,
as its petals are completely gathered.

On the peak of the mountain
a red flag is placed.
Even if rain falls for three years,
the colors won't fade.

From Tibet

In the Islamic world, where this Turkish Mandala originated, the idea exists that there are seven hells, but eight heavenly paradises, for God's justice and scorn are great, but his benevolence and mercy are even greater.

Tibetan texts recall the fact that the number eight expresses a particularly well-balanced completeness that can be found in even the smallest and most insignificant thing.

Ottoman ornament on the gravestone of Sultan Soliman I, Constantinople, Turkey
(beginning of the 16th century) ➤

Robin Hood's Race

Consider:
A stretch of the path already
lies behind you,
another stretch lies still ahead of you.
If you linger
then do so only to fortify yourself,
however, not to give up.

Aurelius Augustinus (St. Augustine, 354–430 C.E.)

This labyrinth symbolizes the woods of Sherwood Forest in which Robin Hood, a friend to the poor, hid himself with his companions. It has four "hiding places," one in each cardinal point where one can fortify oneself and rest. They are marked with crosses in the shape of a sword: on the one hand, as a sign of heavenly protection, and on the other hand, as an expression of the fact that effort and recovery, engagement and retreat, battle and contemplation, belong together.

"Robin Hood's Race," Labyrinth near St. Ann's Well, Sneinton, Nottinghamshire, England
(no longer extant) ➤

The Four Seeds

Silence is not on the peak of the mountains.
Tumult is not in the markets of the cities.
Both are in the heart of Man.

Eastern wisdom

When we retreat into the coloring of Mandalas we do so with the hope of advancing to our own depths. Alone with ourselves, in silence and retreat, it is easier to approach the double meaning of the "grounds" of our life. Only then might we experience ourselves as seeds that are lowered into the ground and thus realize their purpose.

This simple Mandala embodies a sense of reality that is disarmingly simple and unexciting, as it can be found only in very simple things.

Eastern European plate with four husks: the three lines symbolize the power of life. ➤

The Door to the Inner Being

In each human being, there are two aspects: the inner and the outer. There are some people who consume the soul's strengths for the outer human being. These are the people that direct all senses and thoughts to outer and transient goods and do not know anything about the inner human being. This robs the soul of its strength. One must, however, also know that the outer human being can be very active while at the same time the inner one is free and inactive.

It is as with a door: While the main panel of the door, which corresponds to our active part, moves, the hinge on which the entire door hangs remains motionless and is not changed in the least. The hinge—that is the inner human being…

Meister Eckhart, Dominican mystic (1260–1328)

One part swings, another part rests—the experience of coloring of this unusual door-Mandala cannot be better described. It therefore becomes a field of practice for a more relaxed attitude toward life and a harmonious balance between action and contemplation.

Celtic wickerwork, illustration in the Tironic Psalter, Paris (8th century) ➤

Heavenly Sphere Wheel

There come some who talk of things that are great, supernatural, and superglorious, very much as if they had flown above all the heavens, and yet they have never even made a step out of themselves to realize their own nothingness. They might well have come to a reasonable truth, but the vivid truth—which is really truth—is that nobody receives except when on the path of his nothingness.

Johannes Tauler, Dominican mystic (14th century)

The original of this miniature shows two angels setting the outer rows of fixed stars in motion. This consequently drives all the other spheres. The idea of the night sky as a mechanism driven by God can already be found in the Psalms of the Old Testament, the counterpart of non-Jewish religions in which the stars were worshipped as deities. The cross that goes through the circle alludes to the pillars upon which heaven and earth rest (Job, 9:6).

Think about the idea of Heaven as a joyful game of the Creator. Use bright, cheerful colors.

Detail from a miniature, France (14th century) ➤

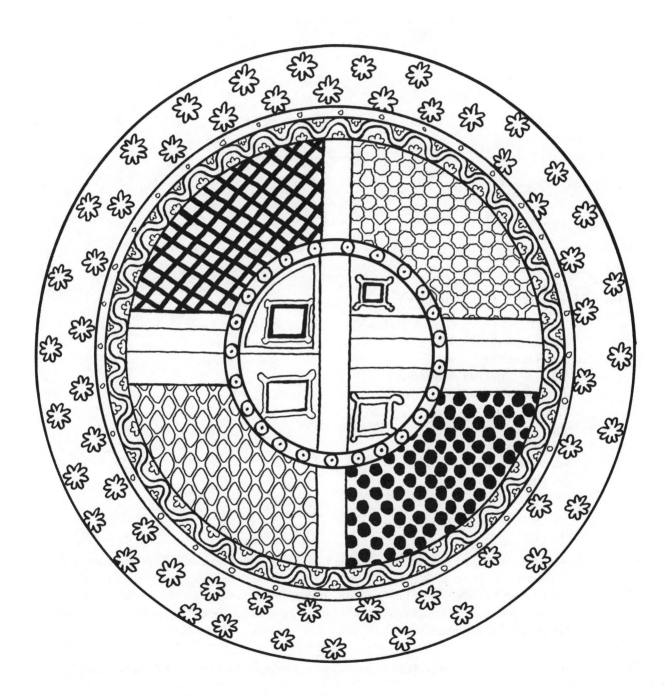

The Feathers of Dignity

Each thing in the universe
returns to its origin.
Returning to the origin means silence.
If one does not recognize the origin
One meets confusion and suffering.
If one recognizes the origin
One becomes patient,
relaxed and clear,
friendly like a grandmother,
dignified as a king.

Lao-tzu *Tao-te-ching* (c. 600 B.C.E.)

This quilt motif with red and green feather bushes was probably designed in connection with the emblem of the Prince of Wales. Ladies who were introduced to the court in the 19th century put gray ostrich feathers in their hair as a sign of adoration and respect for the English crown prince. When coloring the Mandala you might meditate about whom we deem worthy of respect and whom we tend to admire.

"Princess Feather Appliqué," cotton quilt, Vermont, U.S.A. (around 1850) ➤

The Cross of Ravenna

If I were a doctor and someone asked me: what do you think should be done? I would answer: the first thing—the unconditional condition for the fact that anything at all can be done—the first thing that needs to happen is: create silence, help others to silence themselves!

Sören Kierkegaard, philosopher, founder of existentialism (1813–1855)

This ornament contains four half- and four quarter circles besides the one complete circle in the center. However, through the centering around the middle, the "half-way things" of our life likewise gain importance.

When coloring, we see that we are dealing here with a detail of a much greater pattern that could potentially extend in all directions. Thus, the consciousness grows within us that the fragments complement each other and that with each part a greater whole can become possible.

Marble floor from the Byzantine era, San Vitale, Ravenna, Italy ➤

Grass-of-Parnassus

Truly observing a flower, looking inside of it down to the very bottom, we will never come to an end. I cannot get enough of it, from day to day looking at it becomes dearer to me…and I delight ever more in the fact that I engage it with the bottom of my heart. Everything living has its mirror in our soul, and our mind truly absorbs everything if we look at it with love. Then the space in our inner being expands and we ourselves turn into this great flower at last, where all figures and thoughts press around the depth of our soul, like leaves in a great star, around the cup like a deep well…and we become ever more intelligible to ourselves.

Philipp Otto Runge, artist (1777–1810)

The delicately veined, white flower of the grass-of-Parnassus conveys a characteristic amiability that might well be absorbed, especially if we have something eating away at us. In earlier times, the grass-of-Parnassus was considered a cure for liver complaints. If we find ourselves wallowing in the "bog" of negative feelings, it would be a good idea to turn to this Mandala. We may notice when coloring how each part of this flower swells with sympathy and is benevolent toward us— its energy will transfer to us.

Look for other Mandala-shapes outside in nature. If you like, you might take an open or flat bowl and create your very own nature-Mandala on it, using designs of flowers, cones, leaves, and branches.

Inner flower of the marsh grass-of-Parnassus, *parnassia palustris,* according to a photograph by Karl Blossfeldt (1929) ➤

The True Path

A student asked his teacher: "What is the true path?"
The master replied: "The everyday path is the true one."
Once more the student asked: "Can this path be taught?"
The master replied: "The more you learn the more you distance yourself from this path."
Upon this, the student asked: "If you cannot approach the path through studying, how can you recognize it?"
There the master spoke to him: "The path is neither something visible nor something invisible. It is nothing recognizable and nothing unrecognizable either. Do not search for it, do not study it and do not name it. Be open and wide as the sky and you are on the way."

Chao Chou, Zen master (9th century)

East-Asian patterns, such as the Mandala illustrated on the right, are always set up in a strictly geometric fashion. This has the advantage of putting a stop to outer associations. The mind cannot cling to graphic pictures, and our glance becomes free for the "true path," which is neither visible nor invisible.

Japanese silhouette (18th century) ➤

71

Heron

If one deals with Japanese art, then we can see how and with what an indisputably wise man spends his time. Studying the distance of the moon from the earth? No. Studying the politics of Bismarck? No. He studies a single blade of grass. But this blade of grass causes him to paint all plants, then all seasons, the great features of landscapes, then animals, and then the human figure. Thus, he spends his life, and life is too short to carry out everything. Look, is this not almost a true religion that these modest Japanese teach us?

Vincent van Gogh, artist (1853–1890)

Finding simplicity in form and, through this, capturing maximum content: this could be a definition of Japanese art. Each Japanese artist tries to grasp the essence of a plant, an animal, a mountain with as few words or lines as possible. Pictures by Japanese artists convey their beauty through that which is not there. Thus, the suggestions that flow from the picture are given plenty of room, and are able to impact upon the soul of the observer.

Japanese wallpaper motif, Tokyo (19th century) ➤

Rose Window in the Cathedral of Rheims

Nothing should frighten you,
nothing shock you.
God alone remains the same.
The patient one achieves everything,
and whoever has God, has everything.
God alone is enough.

Teresa of Avila, saint (1515–1582)

The divided circle has a definite symbolism: the split wholeness, the differentiation between higher and lower realms, between the visible and the invisible. It is good if the border between the two is thought of as permeable.

Neither of the two halves should fall short nor be devoured by the other one on the path towards maturity in our life. The light side of our soul must not fear the dark side. The unconscious and the conscious may stimulate each other.

The secret theme of this Mandala is the opposition of light and dark. You may express this through strong contrasts—or through the flowing into each other of different shades that lead to the meeting of opposites.

Rose Window in the Cathedral of Rheims, France (first half 13th century)   ➤

The Labyrinth of Lucca

If the pupil were not dark, how then could it receive the divine light?
Hasidic wisdom

The center of this labyrinth is dark. In addition, the path is dark. The limitations that we encounter on our path of life—and which "force" us into one or the other direction—let themselves be colored and meditated upon. The black center point is reminiscent of the black pupil in our eye, of that place where all pictures enter the brain and are put together into an inner picture. A Mandala such as this might encourage us to pass over the world of purely outer pictures and turn our attention to the inside, in order to look through the "blind spot" of the center into that which is real.

Labyrinth on a supporting pillar at the portal of the Cathedral of Lucca, Italy ➤

Ottoman Dome

A human being who wanders in the dark wanders nevertheless. The student learns even if he does not know that he is learning and thus, he might at last get quite excited about it. In winter, a tree collects food. People might think it is idle as they do not see that something is happening. Then in spring they see the buds. Only then do they believe it to be doing something.

There is a time of absorbing and a time of pouring out. This brings us back to the doctrine: "Illumination has to come step by step as otherwise one would be overpowered by the experience."

Jalaluddin Rumi, mystical poet (1207–1273)

This particular Mandala requires time and yet conveys the feeling that there is enough time. It lets us know that we can take our time—even for the smallest details. It teaches the importance of the smallest steps. However, it also teaches that we still move inside the whole, belong to the whole, and serve a whole. It is the wisdom of relaxed advancing that guides us here and which we can take on as our power in everyday life.

Ottoman dome decoration above the tombstone of Sultan Soliman I, Constantinople, Turkey (16th century) ➤

Persian Garden

Yours is nothing beside the hour
in which you live.

Arabic proverb

In a Persian garden, the well is the center. There is no Arab house without a well in the courtyard. As a running water source, the well embodies the essence of all that awakens to life in the garden. The well, or the artistically set up water basin, is both a social gathering point and a silent spot to retire to. Nature arranges itself around it, rests and yet regenerates itself continuously.

Like the other Mandalas, this one is a model for how the world is created through a streaming consciousness that only this hour can make possible.

Persian book illustration, British Museum, London ➤

81

Rose Window in the Cathedral of Milan

If all people have a claim on you, then you yourself may be someone who has a claim on you as well. Why should you be the only one who has nothing of yourself? How much longer will you give your attention to others but not to yourself? Are you perhaps a stranger to yourself? Mustn't you appear strange to others if you appear strange to yourself? He who treats his own person badly, how can he be good?
Thus remember: Don't begrudge yourself.
I do not say: Do this all the time.
I do not say: Do this often.
However, I do say: Do it every once in a while.
Be there for yourself as you are there for others,
or at any rate, be there after all the others.

Bernard of Clairvaux, abbot and mystic (1091–1153)

The dynamic of this Mandala radiates very strongly from its center. As you color, you can experience how much peace rests in the center and how the energy increases as you push ahead to the outside. Nevertheless, it calmly swings back again and again into itself and thus arrrives at a benevolent balance.

Rose window in the apse of the Cathedral of Milan (15th century) ➤

Men and Women of the Earth

Great Spirit,
give us a listening heart:
so that we do not take more from your creation than we give,
so that we do not randomly destroy
only for the sake of our avarice, that we do not refuse
to revive its beauty with our hands,
that we never take from the earth more than
what we really need.
Great Spirit,
give us hearts that understand:
that we cause confusion
when destroying the music of the earth,
that we become blind to its beauty,
when we disfigure its face,
that we have a smelly house
when spoiling its pleasant smell.
Yes, Lord, if we treat the earth with care,
it will care for us.

Native American prayer

Old Native American cultures orient themselves a great deal to the rhythms of nature. They wish to be in harmony with all of creation. They take from nature only as much as they need and strive to give as much in return. Thus arises, in awe of the Great Spirit that penetrates everything, the consciousness of a natural order in which all the experiences of life are stored. Therefore, within each artifact, whether pottered, woven, or braided, the being of the Great Spirit is recognizable to the Native American eye.

Wickerwork on a basket of the Apaches, North America ➤

Vitality

Oh most noble green,
which roots in the sun,
and shines in bright merriment,
in the round of a circling wheel
which does not grasp the glory of the here and now:
embraced by the hearty strength of heavenly secrets,
you glow like the morning light,
and flame like the blazing heat of the sun.
You, green,
are surrounded by love.

Hildegard von Bingen, abbess, writer, composer (1098–1179)

For Hildegard von Bingen, green, or rather viriditas, the green strength, is the basic energy of life. Green "power" is an allegory for the cosmic order, creative energy and the power of procreation, the shining joy of life, and a healthy, wise attitude towards life. If the inner green strength wilts, the human being needs refreshment and recovery in both physical and spiritual respects, where he or she can regenerate much needed strength.

With this Mandala, you can rejuvenate the vitality in your own body.

Plate from Transylvania; the three lines are a symbol of vitality ➤

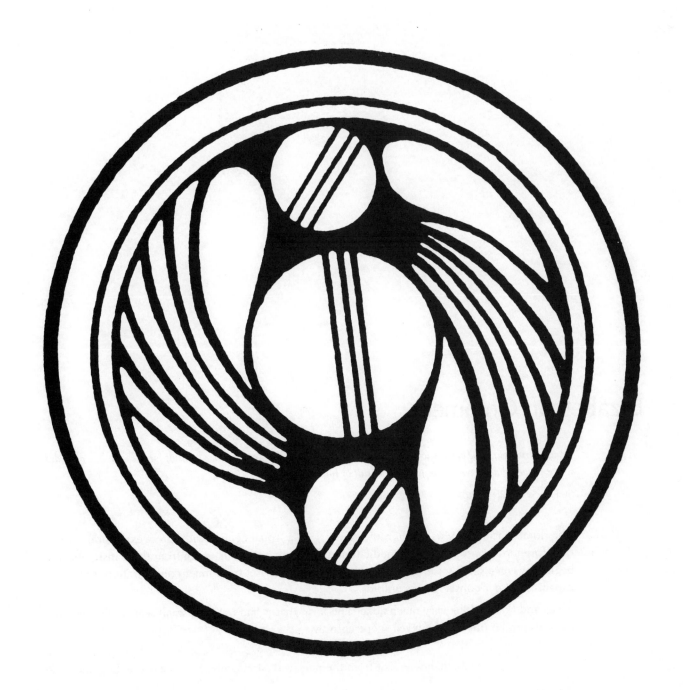

87

Elizabethan Ornament

Let us entrust our good wishes to God and not be worried whether they become fruitful, for He who has awarded us the flower of desire will also give us the fruit of fulfillment.

St. Francis of Sales (1567–1622)

The floral ornament exists through the contrast of a "small center" with "great expansion." It is therefore most appropriate for a meditation upon seeds and fruits, since from these insignificant beginnings on a small scale, great things can arise. Likewise, from inner concentration, the expansion of our consciousness unfolds.

Seeds and flowers look very much alike. The form that is laid out on a small scale multiplies and expands until it fills out the given scope entirely.

Elizabethan woodcut from the palace at Montacute, Somersetshire, England ➤

Butterflies

I, Chuang-tze, dreamt once I was a butterfly, fluttering back and forth, a butterfly in all purposes and goals. I knew only that I followed my moods like a butterfly and was unconscious of ever having been human. Suddenly I awakened and there I lay: "I myself" once more. Now I do not know: Was I then a human being dreaming of being a butterfly or am I now a butterfly dreaming of being human?

Between a human being and a butterfly there is a barrier. To cross it is called transformation.

Chuang-tze (4th century B.C.E.)

In Japan, the motif of the butterfly is used as a sign of particularly lucky moments in life. A bride and groom are given two paper butterflies that will carry the newlyweds on their wings into happiness. Furthermore, moths are worshipped in Asia, since people see the souls of the dead in them, and thus consider them to be the protectors of the living.

This Mandala invites you to recall the happy and sheltered moments in your life, as you color it.

Butterfly *troides hypolitus*, Celebes, Indonesia, according to a photograph
designed as a Mandala   ➤

Alice in Wonderland

"We are all mad here," said the Cheshire Cat ."I'm mad. You're mad."
"How do you know I'm mad?" said Alice.
"You must be," said the Cat, "or you wouldn't have come here."

Lewis Carroll, author, mathematician, and logician (1832–1898)

Alice and the fabled beings from Wonderland are hidden in this crazy labyrinth: the White Rabbit, the Mad Hatter, the Griffon, the Cheshire Cat, the Queen of Hearts…

Alice experiences the wonderland like a maze: the more she tries to understand it, the more she argues with its inhabitants, the more confusing this strange world appears to her—and the more her body size changes. Alice becomes estranged from herself. In the end, a maze like this one teaches that "crazy" experiences can deepen our own path in a peculiar manner and lead to a new, clear viewpoint.

Alice in Wonderland labyrinth, Merritown House, Dorset, England   ➤

93

Double Twist

May the Lord be your friend,
He who gave you the earth
and the sky as a roof above.
May He make your days bright
like the glittering of the spray on the waves,
white as the snow in the mountains,
as the cotton grass in the field,
as the robe of an angel.

From Ireland

You certainly know this: our everyday life with all its demands at work and at home develops a kind of double centrifugal force. Each field rotates and has the tendency to drag us out and away from the center, keeping us extremely busy and sometimes even virtually splitting us. These opposing forces of attraction have enormous power in pulling us toward the outside. Thus, we need to create an opposing movement through our inner force of attraction that brings about tranquility, support, and centering. With this Mandala, we can train the silent forces of our inner being to become strong so that they can bring us back when things are spinning too fast.

Celtic spiral décor, illustration in the *Book of Kells*, Trinity College Library, Dublin, Ireland (9th century) ➤

The Five Senses

The heart is as a water basin, and the five senses are five rivers through which the water pours into the basin from the outside. If you wish clear water to well up from the bottom of the basin, you must remove the water entirely and take out all the black mud that it brought along, and clog all the rivers so that no more water enters. Then dig open the bottom of the basin so that the pure clear water wells up from the interior..

However, as long as the basin is filled with the water that came from the outside, it is impossible for the water to well up from the interior. Thus, also, that knowledge which is supposed to ascend from the interior of the heart cannot well up as long as the heart is not free from all that has entered from the outside.

Ghazali of Tus, Islamic philosopher (1058–1111)

Mandalas can be understood as filtering devices. They separate important matters from unimportant ones, through the power of their turning movement. Many sewage plants for waste water work according to the same principle: through centrifugal force, the heavy substances remain in the center and the lighter ones are washed toward the outside and flushed away.

With the color scheme of this Mandala, we can easily feel the centered force of the spirals. See for yourself how the whirls lead clockwise to the outside and counterclockwise to the center.

Children's book illustration (around 1910)   ➤

Four-Temple Mandala

The yellow emperor wandered once north of the red water, climbed up the slopes of the mountain K'unlun and let his gaze wander towards the south and all over the world. After his return he discovered that he had lost his "dark dull pearl."

He sent out Knowledge to look for it but Knowledge could not find it.

He sent out Perspicacity to look for it but Perspicacity could not find it.

He sent out Conclusiveness to look for it, but Conclusiveness could not find it.

Finally he tried with By-Chance and By-Chance found it.

The yellow emperor said: "How strange that of all people By-Chance was the one capable of finding it!"

Chuang-tze (4th century B.C.E.)

Temple and contemplation have the same linguistic root. Just as believers gather in the temple, the inner forces are collected onto one spot with contemplation. Contemplation means to call on the "inner temple" and to dwell there with care. Neither Knowledge nor Perspicacity open the gates to this holy interior. A certain attentive serendipity, on the other hand, often finds immediate access to the mysterious "pearl" in the innermost part of our hearts.

Can you manage to let go of all intentional creative wishes and self-demands when coloring this Mandala and leave yourself to "By-Chance"?

Mandala on a Tibetan silk scarf (19th century) ➤

Eggshell

Whoever does not grow, will shrink.
I consider it impossible
that love contents itself
by continuously marking the same spot.

Teresa of Avila, saint (1515–1582)

The egg is one of our most favored Easter symbols for the Resurrection. Its quintessence is the new life that is hidden in it and wishes to come to light. The firm shell that is finally smashed protects and conserves this new life only for a very limited time; thus it also embodies in the spiritual sense the "limited horizon" of the human being that is at once outdated and allowed to break apart in order to make possible an even greater growth.

Meditate with the coloring of this 5000-year-old Mandala your own personal possibilities of growth that are "still in the shell." You may also write on the eggs or assign them to certain areas via meaningful signs.

Bowl with egg motif, Mediterranean area (around 3000 B.C.E.) ➤

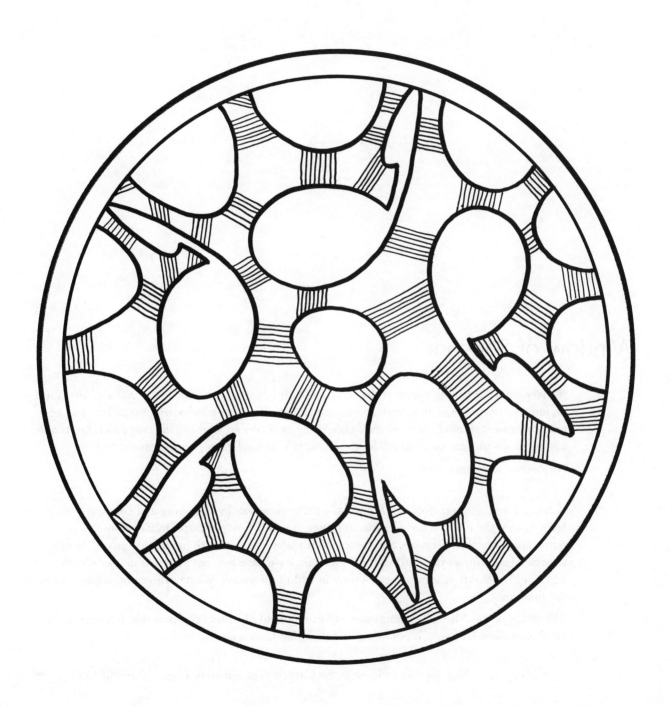

Window of Soissons

It is very difficult to be alone nowadays since there are watches. Have you ever seen a saint with a watch? I could not find one, not even among those saints who are considered patrons of the watchmakers. You see how good we feel in this moment of conversation! We could probably go on like this for years and still have a lot to say to each other. Even after ten years we would still be here, content to be here and still engrossed in conversation.

Pablo Picasso, artist (1882–1973)

When we dedicate ourselves to a Mandala, we take time out. By observing and coloring, we learn to trust the clock inside and also to follow our own very personal inner rhythm. Surprisingly, we also succeed when coloring Mandalas together with others in a group. At first, in need of control, we may still ask how much time we have left, but after a while, we clearly perceive a quite different pulse beat setting in within the group. We have given ourselves over to our inner time.

The image of this Mandala reminds some of us of a kind of natural compass that has been decorated with floral elements. It points out the time that has accrued to us.

New Gothic window in the Cathedral of Soissons, France (around 1850) ➤

Four-Fold Knot

There were once two monks who read together in an old book that there was a place at the end of the world at which heaven and earth touched and God's Kingdom began. They decided to look for it and not to return until they found it. They wandered across the world, survived innumerable dangers, suffered all kind of privations that wandering across the world demands and all distractions that could lead human beings away from their goal. A door was supposed to be there, or so they had read. They had only to knock and they would be in God's Kingdom. At last, they found what they had been looking for. They knocked at the door and with trembling heart they watched as it opened. When they entered, they were standing at home in their monastery cell. They looked at each other and then they understood: the place at which God's Kingdom on earth begins is at the spot God has assigned to us.

Source unknown

It is an ancient rite in many cultures to place yourself first in a north-south and then in a west-east direction. Thus, in dance or meditative silence, all four cardinal points can be "grasped." The energy of wholeness can be felt in the polarity of two directions.

This Celtic wicker pattern is reminiscent of such rites. The forms, which might appear confusing at first, eventually, with longer observation, dissolve into two structures that are twisted by 90 degrees. Therefore, this figure is well-suited to bring about clarity and reorientation in times of confusion.

Celtic wicker pattern on a sacramentary (book for the liturgy) in the Cathedral of Rheims, France (12th Century) ➤

Mandala from Nishapur

The end of knowledge is
that man comes to the point
where he was at the beginning…

Abu Yazid al-Bistami, Sufi saint (800–875)

If one bent line meets another, and does not hit it at a right angle, the two lines should approach each other until they merge. This basic principle can be found everywhere in nature. The Oriental cultures that have chosen flower and leaf motives as models strictly adhere to this idea. Such agreements with nature give an immediate charm to the ornaments art historians call the "melody of form." Together with another principle, that of "returning asymmetry," it lets arise such dynamic, heart-shaped structures as those pictured. Thus, refrain and melody come together.

Listen for the melodies of this Mandala that resound with each repetition, though with slight variations.

Stucco paneling from Nishapur, Iran (10th century) ➤

The Sun of Both Worlds

There are two suns:
One shines on the earth, the other on the soul.
That which shines on the earth drives away the darkness,
the other, which shines on the soul, drives away fear.
When one rises, the celestial bodies fade;
when the other rises, bonds vanish.
Yet the sun is indivisible in its brightness;
it neither belongs to the people,
nor are they worthy of it.
Each one of them will be blessed with it according to the degree of his rank.
He who delights in observing it with his own eye,
is awarded with the sight of the sun;
he who delights in the sun watching him,
will be delighted with the eternal glance.

From Persia

This sun pulsates from its hot core and sets its incredible energy free in different spheres. Anyone who loves the stimulating feeling of the sun's rays on bare skin, knows how much positive energy can be set free in us through light and warmth. In winter, our inner sun thirsts for the outer one. In spiritual consciousness, the reverse is true: the meditating person learns that the outer sun only waits for the inner sun to start shining.

This Mandala helps to activate our own inner charisma. In addition, the symbol of the sun mobilizes hope, pure intentions, and love of truth.

Baroque scheme from Robert Fludd, *Utriusque Cosmi (Both Worlds)*,
Alchemical tradition (1619) ➤

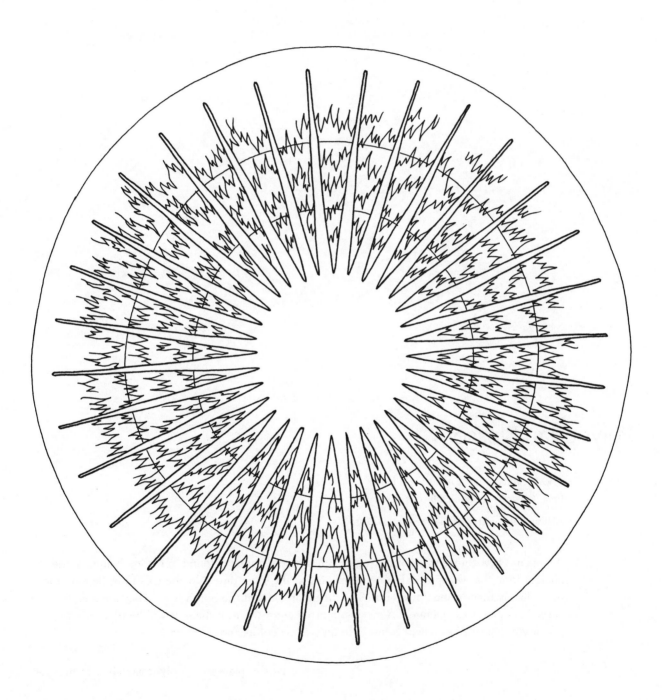

Polynesian Blossom

The vegetative universe opens like a flower
from the earth's center: in which is eternity.

William Blake, poet, artist, and mystic (1757–1827)

Art creates new things by reproducing in a new manner what is found in nature. Nature is the ancient form that we approach by withdrawing at the same time. Nowhere can this be felt more immediately than in the flower motifs of the inhabitants of the South Seas. They are unconcerned and never exaggerated. A merry atmosphere grows from them. It will be transferred to you if you trace these ancient forms with only a few colors and fill them in.

Flower plate from Polynesia, fabric print ➤

Angel Mandala

Behold, I send an angel before you,
to guard you on the way
and bring you to the place
which I have prepared.

Exodus 23.20–21

The four cross-bearing angels are probably the four archangels Michael, Gabriel, Raphael, and Uriel. Since ancient times, angels have been considered companions of man, representatives of the Divine, messengers of transcendence. Whenever angels meet a human being, the latter becomes aware of the presence and closeness of God. The most widespread belief is that we are under the protection of a very specific angel who stands by our side.

At such time as you wish to place yourself or another human being under divine protection, this angel Mandala will do you good.

Ascension of the Cross, Byzantine façade décor from Kazchi, Georgia (11th Century) ➤

Ashanti

From each point of the circle to the center runs a footbridge,
a path, from the greatest error back to God.
Whichever heart still loves something, is not alone
as one little fiber is enough to take root in God.

Friedrich Rückert, poet (1788-1866)

Manifold symbols of numbers pass through this simple décor: in the center a ten-rayed star, surrounded by an eleven-edged wreath of rays. From it, five paths lead with nine steps each towards the outside and seven waves each fill the space in between. It can remain open whether each number has a greater significance or not. This figure therefore gets its appeal from the sheer variety of numbers it contains.

The African always experiences him- or herself in the community, and thus the manifold elements of this carving work could be understood as a kind of conversion of this communal experience.

With Mandalas like these, you may sensuously experience numbers when coloring. In addition, new connections can be established with the colors. Freely associate what you feel with the individual numbers. This Mandala is also very well suited as a coloring experience for two.

Ashanti Messing lid décor, Ghana, Africa ➤

Three Leaves

Blessed maple leaves!
Lovely is the brilliance
and then comes the fall.

Japanese Haiku

Mandalas always encompass the very great experiences of life—death, as well. "Becoming lovely" as a preparation for fading is a natural process. In English, the fruit-bearing season is therefore called Fall—the time of falling. What comes to your mind in this respect? What has fallen to you? What would you like to see fall?

The leaves of this Mandala can be colorfully arranged in such a way that different levels of autumnal fullness, of transition, and detachment all become visible at once.

Décor at a well, Wells, England (Middle Ages) ➤

Persian Wheel

We human beings, captured by Your perfect beauty, see on all horizons nothing but Your obvious sign...
From a Persian prayer

In Islam, one must adhere strictly to the prohibition from the Old Testament against icons. The scripture plays therefore an even greater role for Muslims. The more artistically the 99 names of God or text sections of the Koran have been integrated in an ornament, the greater is the merit of the artist, according to Islamic belief. Calligraphists (designers of scriptures) therefore deserve the greatest esteem.

"Islam" means "devotion," and with this Mandala you can devote yourself to the experience of sacred signs that you might not be able to read directly, but can still understand intuitively as an expression of human devotion.

Painted bowl, Islamic, Nishapur (10th century) ➤

Moon Disks

The moon is,
since its light produces fertile moisture,
amiable towards young animals
and budding plants.
Indeed are the deeds of the moon,
deeds of reason and complete wisdom.

Plutarch, priest, philosopher, writer (c. 120 C.E.)

In the course of a month, the moon changes its shape several times. We can watch its silvery crescent waxing or waning. We can observe the new moon and experience the subtly shining full moon. With its versatility, the moon is assigned to the female body and its cycles. Under its sign, many deities ruled who awarded female beauty and virtue to women, gave them fertility, and assisted them during childbirth. As the light of the night and the unconscious, the mildly shimmering disk also embodies the feminine aspects of the personality of men.

During the time of your own change and transition or in a "weak" phase, you may open up to your own "lunar consciousness" with this Mandala.

Traditional ornament with waxing and waning moon disk, West Africa (19th century) ➤

Net of the Mamelukes

I, your Lord, was a hidden treasure
and craved being recognized;
therefore, I created the earth.

Hadith of the Prophet Muhammad (570–632)

On the way to a new present, we must leave behind old nets. In order to do so, however, we must first recognize them. Often they are invisible, hidden: the net of habits that have come to a standstill, the nets of a value system that is all too rigid, the net of deceptive self-assessments… There are also nets that hold the body, the spirit, and the soul captive. And there are networks that protect and conserve life, that provide stability and bring about firm connections, but are, nevertheless, elastic and nonrestrictive.

Discover with this Islamic Mandala your own very personal network experiences.

Koran cover, Mameluken tradition, Cairo, Egypt (14th century) ➤

The Serpent

One is everything,
with it is everything,
in it is everything.
The snake is the one.
It has two symbols,
good and evil.

From a Greek tract (11th century)

The snake that bites its own tail is called "ouroborus." "Ouro" means "king" in Coptic, and "ob" means "snake" in Hebrew. In alchemical writings, the ouroborus is a symbol of the world spirit, which decides upon life or death and can take on all forms. Thus it is, at the same time, everything and nothing. Also in our dreams, the snake appears as an ambiguous symbol of transcendence. It frightens us, yet it can —especially as a white or golden snake—also bring about cures and integration.

Baroque book illustration, Amsterdam (17th century)   ➤

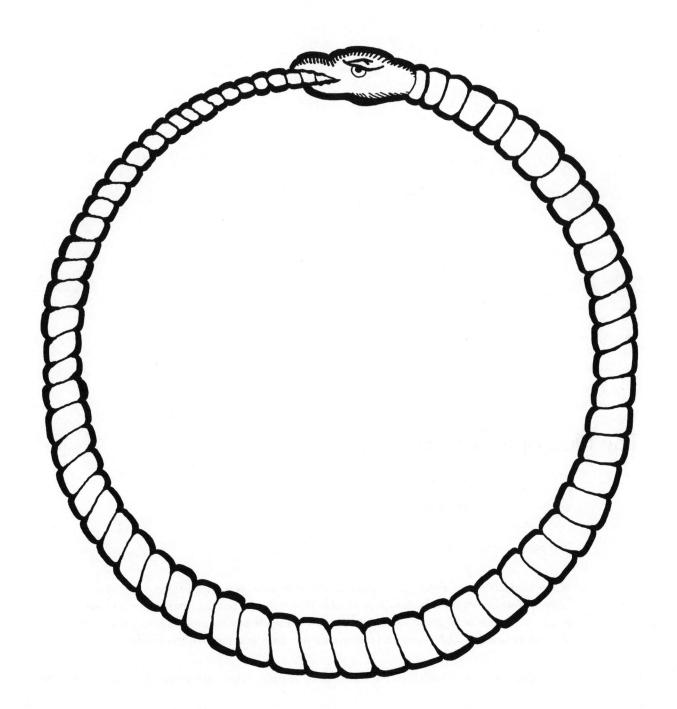

The Blossoms of Cairo

In creation lies mystery,
which like a spring suddenly pours forth—
on and on.

From Sufism, Islamic mysticism

In the Mandala on the right, the ceremonial blossom ornaments dance around a mysterious center. Creation is a mystery, says this Arabian flower dance, but one that can be revealed, at one point, as a source of all being—perhaps less through intellectually picking it to pieces than through honoring it and learning to understand ourselves as a piece of the mystery.

Arabian ornament from light embossed white marble, from a private residence in Cairo ➤

126

Rock Flower

We do not know,
how the stonebreak
cracks rock.
It practices its art
in its way
and without noise. God
loves the quiet.

Karl Heinrich Waggerl, illustrator and author (1897–1973)

In Germany the stonebreak (saxifrage) was considered a plant with wondrous strength. With its location high in the mountains "near the clouds," and its ability to cling to the rocks even in dark chasms, it seemed to have a mysterious, "eternal" strength. The plant can indeed break up stone floors, and thus, pick up the minerals essential for life.

This Mandala also has its own power of resistance and its own energy that we can mobilize for meditation.

Clustered stonebreak, based on a photograph by Karl Blossfeldt,
"Archetypes of Art" (1929) ➤

129

The Palace of the Nine Paths

Confucius said, "I would prefer not speaking."
Then said his student, Tsze-kung: "If you, Master, do not speak, what shall we, your students, record?"
The Master said," Does Heaven speak? And nevertheless the four seasons pursue their courses and all creatures come into being, but does Heaven say anything?"

Confucius, philosopher (551–479 B.C.E.)

Squares and circles are the themes of this Mandala. The square is the symbol of the world, the earthly totality. The circle is the epitome of perfection and represents, therefore, the world of the divine. Pictures such as these ask that the worldly in us be allowed to mature into the divine. The original Mandala has given a part of the square very dark colors, and through them, expresses the idea that we can realize our totality only by becoming conscious of our darker sides.

If you set out on the search for yourself in this Mandala, think of the following: that seen from the middle the problematic aspects of our personality are still a part of the whole, even though we prefer to ignore them and try to drive them out.

Mandala for going deeper, Udaipur, Rajasthan, India (18th century) ➤

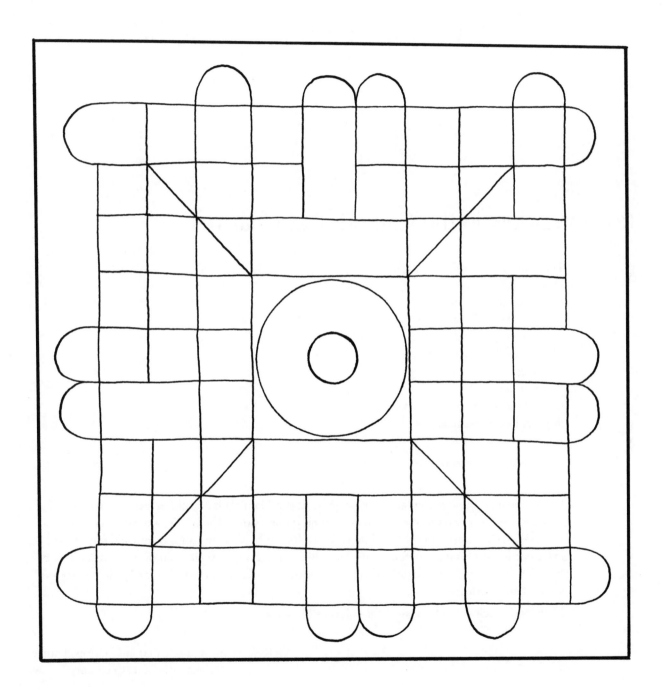

Rose Window in the Cathedral at Chartres

Those who wish to begin a good life,
should do it as
they would draw a circle.
If they set the middle point
correctly and it is fixed,
then the line of the circle is good.
This means:
If humans learn first
to let their heart remain firmly in God,
they will then become steady
in all their works.

Meister Eckhart, Dominican mystic (1260–1328)

Oddly enough, the representation of elements in the Mandala has nothing monotonous or tiring about it. On the contrary: the recurrence, when it comes from the inside, appears ingenious and necessary. If it is born from the middle, and not forced by strange hands or outside powers, it makes possible a high measure of spiritual stability. Rituals gain their strength from reliable symbols. The recurring circle form in this rose window from Chartres is a plea for stable energy and strengthening effects.

Have you developed a firm ritual for coloring Mandalas?

Rose Window, cathedral at Chartres, France
(1st half of the 13th century) ➤

Yorkshire Labyrinth

We find God most certainly in our inner self.

Meister Eckhart, Dominican mystic (1250–1328)

Each labyrinth, as mysteriously entwined as it may be, has an entrance. Labyrinths open themselves for searchers, who are open to the unexpected. Wherever the path may lead, we can find
it only if we bring with us an openness and are ready to face uncertainty. This labyrinth is
shaped round like an "O," the first letter of openness. Openness is, so to speak, the red thread of
Ariadne, which winds through this labyrinth and opens the way.

Labyrinth from Ripon Common North Yorkshire, England, today destroyed   ➤

Sumerian Seal

Make it so that I become solidly united with you;
Like a seal on a letter, so that when one wants
to take the seal off, one must tear the letter;
So that when I should be separated from you,
we would have to be ripped apart,
so that not even the sway of death can keep us apart forever.
So place me in your heart!
So take me in your arms!
Do not merely clasp me, but rather hold me!
Dig yourself in! Remain attached!
Do not let me loose again!

Niklaus Ludwig Graf von Zinzendorf, reformer (1700–1760)

Would you want to make mistakes—intentionally? With their sand-Mandalas and carpet-weavings, many Native Americans traditionally and quite consciously work a "mistake" into their pattern, so that the Great Spirit can much more easily penetrate it. The imperfection of their work allows them to leave perfection to God alone and to deal more calmly with themselves and with others. Perfection often lacks a certain lively harmony, which arises through the permission for, and acceptance of, slight irregularities.

This, the most ancient dated Mandala in the book, is about 6,000 years old. In its archaic structure are irregularities and quite a few "mistakes." So "what is missing"—that which is not yet in us—may more easily come to us.

Sumerian seal with cross-shaped motif, Susa (around 4000 B.C.E.) ➤

Gold—the Element

Journey! You will find a replacement for the one you leave behind. Neither glory nor skill lie in quiet staying, but rather in travel and action.

The calm, undisturbed surface of the water becomes stagnant, if the wind does not set it in motion. If, however, the wind rages upon it, the water becomes good.

If the sun stayed stationary in the firmament, it would soon become a burden to the inhabitants of the earth. If the lion did not leave the forest, it would very seldom find prey; and if the arrow did not leave the bow, it would never find its mark.

If gold remained forever in the mines, then it would not be as highly regarded as it is, and the exquisite aloe wood if kept in its own country would be considered only a kind of wood—like any other.

From *A Thousand and One Nights*

The desire for gold has set thousands upon thousands of people in motion and led them to become treasure hunters. The vast majority sought real treasure; only a few among them understood it as a search for the highest value of the inner personality, which rewards every difficulty with an inner search. The real as well as the inner gold is hidden. It must be found, exposed, and extracted with effort. This golden Mandala brings everything that you imbue with the highest value closer to you—a treasure of true gold, a golden heart, the golden age, and also the highest dignity, love, mercy, God.

Just a design tip for this Mandala: Perhaps a part of your gold lies still hidden under dark colors, flashing through, however, here and there? After coloring it, if you wish, you could highlight the lines in addition with a fine gold-colored pencil or inscribe a couple of precious personal words.

Flat representation of Gold (Element 79) ➤

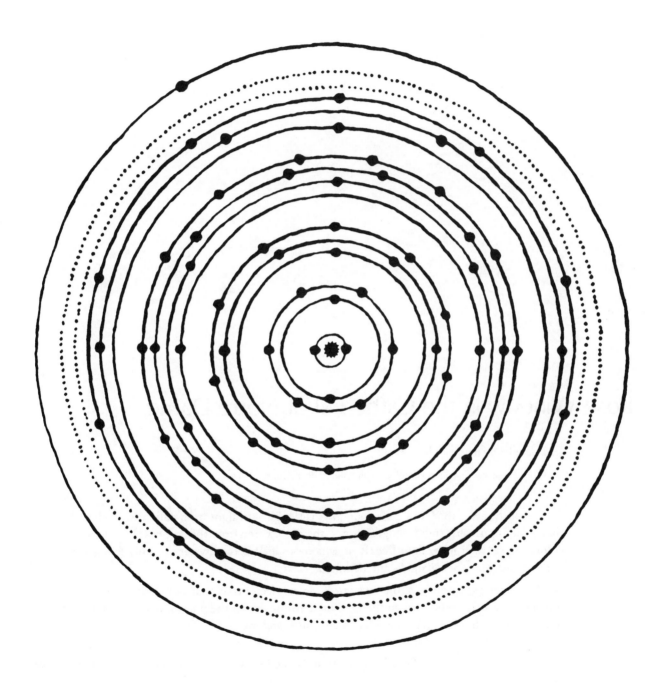

139

Rose Window in the Cathedral of Notre Dame

God works in the innermost heart of all.

St. Thomas Aquinas, Dominican theologian and philosopher (1225–1274)

The great theme of the Gothic rose windows is the birth of light from darkness. With a gleam that we know usually only from gemstones, they break free from the darkness with their radiant colors and set their inner light free. Rose windows speak of the mystery of truly living and shining from our inner being amidst the darkness.

As human beings, we all have the mysterious power deep inside that can let us shine; that will not allow our light to be extinguished, no matter how dismal the phases that we undergo. When it breaks through, we experience it like a new birth and mercy.

Rose Window from Notre Dame Cathedral, Paris (around 1250) ➤

Disk from Bashikah

Whoever has watched himself, will then—when he watches—watch himself as someone who has become simple. Or better said: he will simply be connected with himself and simply feel himself...He becomes, so to speak, another; he stops being himself, he no longer belongs to himself. Having arrived at this point, he has been taken up into God and has become one with Him, as a center point that coincides with another center point.

Plotinus, Greek philosopher (204–270 C.E.)

Simplicity is a wonderfully uncomplicated prescription to relieve the soul. It makes contemplation of the Real possible and therefore produces a great sense of coherence. It is an ancient experience that noble simplicity is highly welcome after difficult and complicated phases in life. Simplicity comforts. "Now things are simpler again," means more or less "now everything is good again."

To the right is an uncomplicated, easy to grasp Mandala with simple motifs that meet exactly in the middle. It serves children as well as adults who are burdened with stress.

Glazed tile, Assyria, Bashikah, Mesopotamia (around 700 B.C.E.) ➤

Three Double-Headed Dragons

As you were in the beginning,
when the good world arose,
so be turned towards me every day.

As you were in the beginning,
when my path began,
so be with me each mile.

As you were in the beginning,
when you shaped my soul,
so hold me in your hands
until my end.

From Ireland

The ancient mythological motif of the World Dragon embodies the experience of the chaotic in the individual. The "inner dragon" often sleeps long in the darkness; however, it can emerge suddenly and dangerously threaten the mental balance of the person.

The woven bands in this Mandala control the three double-headed Chaos Dragons. In the light of consciousness, the unleashed darkness and chaotic power are conquered. The dragon through the central, symmetrical order of the sun disk is "overcome" and integrated.

Celtic illustration from the *Book of Kells*, Trinity College Library, Dublin, Ireland
(beginning of the 9th century) ➤

The Four Seasons

Everything that the power of the world does takes place in a circle. The heavens are round, and I have heard that the earth is round like a ball, and so are all the stars. The wind, if it unfolds its greatest force, forms whirls. The birds build themselves round nests, for their religion is the same as ours. The sun comes out from under and goes down once more in a circle. The moon does the same. And both are round. Even the seasons form their alternating course in a great circle and always return there, from whence they have come. A person lives in a circle from childhood to childhood, and so it goes with everything in which the power moves. Our tepees were round like birds' nests, and they were always set up in a circle, the ring of a people, a nest of many nests, where the Great Spirit wished us to care for our children.

Black Stag

The four seasons form the great nature Mandala, in which the creation carries out its great cycle. Each season arises from the previous one and lives on in the following. The four seasons are wonderful spiritual leaders. Those who meditate upon the changes of Becoming and Fading in nature also learn to deal more consciously with these processes in their own life. They perceive themselves as truly taking part in a cycle, in which nothing gets lost and power propels time and again.

With this Native American Mandala, you can express other four-fold experiences as well: four different times of the day, four different phases of your life, four different aspects of an object, four different sides of your personality...

Native American symbol of the four seasons, North America ➤

Indian Mandorla

Center of all centers, core of cores,
Almond, which closes itself tightly and sweetens, —
This entire world out to all the stars
is the fruit of your flesh: Hail.

Rainer Maria Rilke, poet (1875–1926)

A fluid light-wreath or halo in the shape of an almond is called a "Mandorla." In the sweet core lies the exquisite mystery of the almond, hidden, well-wrapped and protected with a solid shell.

At the same time, the Mandorla marks a circle that has an above and a below. Many old portrayals of Christ as sovereign of the world show him in a Mandorla, in order to link the symbol of the all encompassing circle of the earth with the saying, "As in Heaven, so on Earth."

Those who look at or color this Mandorla will feel as if they stretch toward Heaven and Earth. In the middle, one discovers the individual sweet core, the individual tenderness, and the individual yearning: shown here is a unique lotus blossom, which surpasses all surrounding blossoms in size and beauty.

Indian Mandorla from a book jacket, lacquer painting, India House, London
(18th century) ➤

Star of Arabia

Just as a shape is reflected in tiny pieces of a broken mirror, so the beauty of true unity of being is mirrored in the clearly different planes of existence.

Arabian wisdom

Even so simple a Mandala as this brings about a new feeling for the inner unity of many individual parts. The longer our gaze lingers there, the more we can perceive the unity through the great variety of the individual triangles and squares.

This Mandala obtains its energy entirely from its inner unity and releases it outward very harmoniously.

Mystic diagram for the improvement of contemplation, Arabic ➤

Demon

The great painter Salvador Dali was once asked what he would take out of the Louvre first in case of a fire. His answer was, "The fire."

From a radio interview

Since the Mandalas embrace the entirety of reality, they enclose darker parts as well. This demon was exorcised into the circle; now his destructive power becomes visible, though, at the same time, also restricted and confined. Perhaps you can assign to this demon your own fiery energies when coloring the Mandala, such as the spirit of opposition, criticism, combativeness, aggression, rage, and so on.

Like the Tibetan, the Native American Sand Mandalas were destroyed immediately after their completion, proceeding from the assumption that the content of the Mandala had been completely absorbed into the interior of the person who formed it. The destruction, in this instance, is a sensible letting go of the visionary and spiritual preoccupation with the Mandala.

If you wish, you may burn your finished Mandala and observe how the fire feeds from the center to the edge. The destroyed Mandala will certainly remain in your memory.

Demon in serpent form, Latin America ➤

Shou from Kyoto

A Monk asked the Master: "Show me the path without words."
Spoke the Master: "Ask me without words!"

Zen saying

A very simple and symmetrical Mandala, like that on the right-hand page, attracts attention. It focuses energy, brings it back from dispersion. At the same time, it demands that we become very conscious of its lines. As an exercise to develop such care, this Japanese silhouette can help us to perceive just that which is truly there.

Through painting, we can clearly illuminate our thoughts and feelings with this Mandala and get away from the shadow of false ideas.

Shou motif, Silhouette, Kyoto, Japan ➤

155

Shield from Khorsabad

If it were only once so very still.
If Chance and Accident
fell silent and the neighboring laughter,
if the noise, which my senses make,
did not prevent me so well from watching—:

Then could I, in a thousandfold thought,
imagine you up to the very edge of you
and possess you (if only for a long smile),
in order to give you away to all life
as a sign of gratitude.

Rainer Maria Rilke, poet (1875–1926)

Mandalas are "Shields of Stillness" against the noise and stress of our everyday lives. Circle after circle, we can shield ourselves and create a protective defense against all the rush and bustle from the outside as well as the inside. Through concentrated stillness, the Mandala trains our mental defenses and awakens a healthy spiritual "battle energy." A special kind of vigilance—clear and certain—goes hand in hand with this energy.

Color this Mandala, depending on your need, in soft shades that will shield you, or with clear, strong tones that represent your inner "battle energy."

Assyrian-Persian décor from a royal bronze shield, Khorsabad, Iraq
(presumably 9th century B.C.E.) ➤

Quilt from Hawaii

What lived there,
which from a narrow circle
strove out to Infinity,
gentle and quiet
sank back into itself
and swelled up in unconscious happiness.

Friedrich Hebbel, author (1813–1863)

The volcanic island group of Hawaii is about 18 million years old. Every 70,000 years or so, a new species of plant came to the lava islands, with the help of the wind or carried over the ocean by birds. Through mutation and a lack of natural enemies, nature allowed countless new species to come into being, which are to be found nowhere else on earth. On Hawaii, it is said, the flowers "sing": at least they explode in brilliant colors, exotic shapes, and entrancing fragrances.

With this Hawaiian Mandala, we can meditate upon the wealth of creative events, that took place in inconceivable calm over a period of millennia.

"Exotic Bloom," cotton quilt, Hawaii, U.S.A. (circa 1930)   ➤

Tibetan Mandala

Outside the cup is white.
Inside the milk is white.
In the middle the individual heart is white.
United, the three whites are a good sign.

If I should tell, whether the thoughts are pure,
this I say, they are as milk in the cup.
If I should say, whether the knowing heart is in harmony,
this I say, it is as the tiny key to the small box.

From Tibet

This Tibetan Mandala embodies the cosmic plan in the structure of a well consolidated, heavenly palace. Four entrances or palace gates surround the inner lotus, the dwelling of the godhead. In the center live purity and wisdom. According to the Tibetan imagination, we find ourselves with our own entry into the Mandala "on the other side of time." The systematic structure of this type of Mandala establishes a comprehensive order, which is strong enough to assert itself against destructive powers and to withstand opposition.

When coloring, we can emphasize this idea by using strongly contrasting colors for the opposing color fields and creating a bright center.

Tibetan Mandala in the shape of a heavenly palace (19th century)   ➤

In the Name of the Rose

The red rose belongs to the splendor of Allah.
Whoever would like to see His splendor, should look at the red rose.

Muhammad, prophet (570–632)

The much beloved queen of flowers is also an ancient mystical symbol. Its grace and beauty, its richness in form, its intense fragrance, the fullness of its petals, which enclose a mysterious inside, bestow a magic upon the rose that hardly anyone can evade. The flower, which represents the happiness of love, carries, however, thorns as well, and therefore also presents grievous experiences in the fulfillment of love. Thus it becomes a symbol of life for many mystics, whose love for God and for people was not destroyed through sorrowful experiences, but rather matured even more.

This Mandala elevates the rose to a representation of the "summum bonum," the highest good, the splendor of God, which unfolds within us and around us.

Robert Fludd, *Summum Bonum* (*The Highest Good*) (1629) ➤

163

Clay Disk of the Anasasi

We call upon the earth, our home planet,
We call upon the mountains, the peaks of stillness,
We call upon the waters, which flow through the earth,
And implore: teach us and show us the way.
We call upon the land, on which our food grows,
We call upon the forests, which reach to the heavens,
We call upon the animals of the prairies, which are as we at home here,
And implore: teach us and show us the way.
We call upon everyone who has lived here upon this earth,
We call upon everyone whom we love,
We call upon the Great Spirit, who flows throughout the entire universe,
And implore: teach us and show us the way.

Prayer of the Chinook Indians

The wisdom of Native Americans grows out of their capacity for feeling themselves a part of a benevolent Whole. Thus they can ally themselves like siblings with these forces that unfold in creation. They are open to visible as well as invisible connections that exist between all aspects of nature, and are able to use them as a special source of power. Thus they develop an assured instinct for their own way of living on the planet.

Native American pottery, New Mexico, U.S.A. ➤

Apsis from Bourges

God is eternally ready,
but we are very unprepared;
God is near to us,
but we are distant from Him;
God is inside,
we are outside;
God is at home in us,
we are in exile.

Meister Eckhart, Dominican mystic (1260–1328)

The paired idea of "inside" and "outside" is characteristic of each cathedral. Through the artistic doubling of the half-circular final vestibule of the nave, arises the basic shape of a building that is oriented completely toward the middle. Each movement toward the middle is a step inward.

When coloring this Mandala, let the walls rise above the outline before your spiritual eye. Imagine the cupola, which curves between columns, and draw the colors that result from the play of light in the room. You will notice that you are hovering above the paper at the beginning, as the architect, so to speak. At the end, you will find yourself in the center of the floor once more, admiring the beauty of your own cathedral.

Mandala, developed from the reflective floor plan of the apsis of the cathedral in Bourges, France (1194–1260) ➤

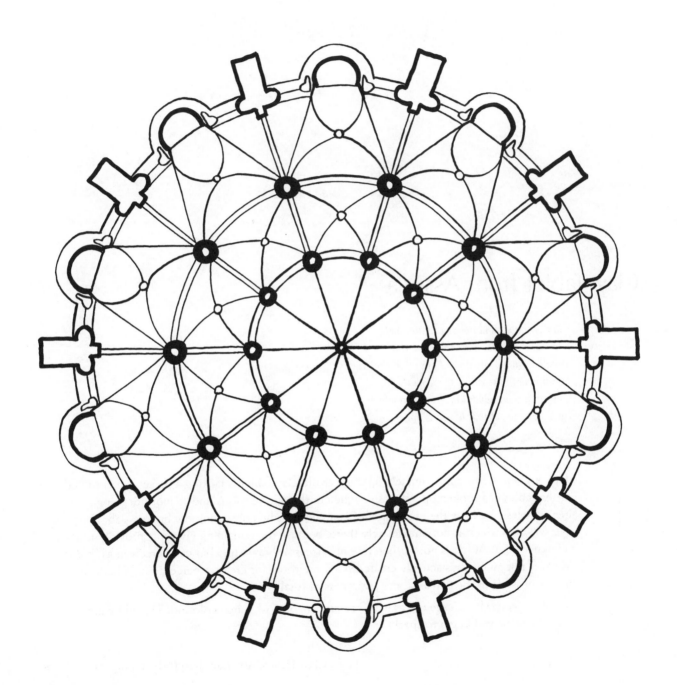

167

Clay Tablet from Assyria

Clay is shaped and hollowed into a pot.
What is not there makes the pot useful.
Windows and doors are cut out when constructing a room.
What is not there makes the room useful.
Thus pull your advantage from that which is,
by making use of that which is not.

Lao tzu, *Tao-te-ching* (c. 600 B.C.E.)

The original of this approximately 3,000-year-old clay tablet is lacking a piece—an entire edge of the tablet had broken off. (It was completed, though, in this Mandala motif drawing.) Nevertheless, we have the impression of completion when observing the broken slab. Our inner eye sees that which is not immediately there, because the remaining elements provide sufficient references to it. What is not, is therefore not necessarily missing, but can perceived as "hidden." What is not might thus actually create even more room for creative perception. What is not makes possible in the end a greater awareness of totality.

So, allow yourself to leave out as many details as you wish when coloring. The white areas of your Mandala will begin to speak!

Fired Clay Tablet, Assyrian, Iraq (9th century B.C.E.) ➤

Labyrinth from St. Quentin

Even the longest journey
begins with a single step.
Fear not
the slow forward movement,
Fear only
remaining still.

From China

As with many tales, there are three different possibilities in this labyrinth that can lead to the finish. The outer border opens three times. From each of these points, we can look for the correct path to the center. The "true" path is, as you will quickly notice, given in the black lines. While you progress onward with the colors, you will shape the experience on both sides of the inner paths. You can blend the chosen colors, layer them into one another, or, for each new step or new thought on the path, set a new contrasting color. Experiment with short and long color lines, and trust in your creative freedom, which "as if all by itself" will find new innovative paths.

Floor labyrinth in the Cathedral of St. Quentin, France ➤

St. Vigean's Knot

Lord, bless the first day and the last.
Bless the hours which are not begrudged to me.
My hands should bless
what they touch.
My ears should bless
what they hear.
My eyes should bless
what greets them.
May a blessing come from my lips.
May my neighbor be blessed;
May he also bless me!
Lord, leave me not out of your eyes,
your hands, your ears, your heart.
On this day and all the days of the year.

From Ireland

For the Celts, the stone was the "body" of the earth and therefore a powerful embodiment of greatness. This knot in stone thus arose from the approximation of a bodily experience: those respectfully entwining arms, crossing one another, are an ancient gesture of prayer. This centers us, leads us back to ourselves, and mobilizes our inner power, which reaches its full expression in the picture of the powerful knot. This lively and at the same time binding power will be experienced as a blessing and passed on.

When coloring it, follow how your own individual powers of body, soul, and spirit will be pleasantly entwined through this Mandala.

Celtic circular ornament on the foot of the stone cross in the churchyard of St. Vigean, Angusshire, Scotland ➤

Japanese Silhouette

Glory be to God for dappled things—
For skies of couple-colour as a brinded cow;
For rose-moles all in stipple upon trout that swim;
Fresh-firecoal chestnut-falls; finches' wings;
Landscape plotted and pieced—fold, fallow, and plough;
And áll trádes, their gear and tackle and trim.
All things counter, original, spare, strange;
Whatever is fickle, freckled (who knows how?)
With swift, slow; sweet, sour; adazzle, dim;
He fathers-forth whose beauty is past change:
Praise Him.

Gerard Manley Hopkins, poet and Jesuit priest (1844–1889)

A great deal of patchwork from many small points, elongated fields, and oddly shaped flecks display themselves here before the eyes of the observer. And yet we have no difficulty in seeing the whole amidst various things. The whole always has a place for wonderful shapes and variety. Its beauty is truly founded, above all else, upon the magnificent capability for integration.

Where we succeed in respecting the smallest detail and nonetheless approach the whole, something completely new emerges from the middle, as does the splendid blossom here from the leaf ring.

Blossom, Japanese Silhouette (19th century) ➤

Gotlandish Whirl-Wheel

Having home in oneself! How different would life be!
It would have a center, and from that center all powers would emerge.
However, thus my life has no center,
but is rather suspended twitching
between many lines and poles and counterpoles.

Hermann Hesse, author (1877–1962)

There are conceptions that whirl, as with this motif, representing planets, which revolve about the sun in a round dance. The spiral motion is a central element in cultic dances with contrasting poles such as life and death, or waxing and waning.

Take this Mandala as an invitation to participate in a cosmic dance around the resting center. When coloring, enjoy your own rhythm and the changes of quick and slow, inner and outer, coming and going, rotating and resting.

Cult stone with sun motif from Gotland, Sweden (pre-Christian era) ➤

Japanese Lacquer Flower

Then the blossoms fall.
Only quiet now prevails
in the human soul.

Japanese haiku

The art of giving objects a lacquer surface has been around for 3,000 years. In Asia, this has been brought to mastery. Many thin layers are put on in such a way that a highly brilliant surface arises. It reflects light very well, although it is itself colored darkly. Lacquer cabinets or boxes reflect light even in semidarkness or with a little candlelight. This gives the objects a somewhat mysterious, mystical quality.

Would you like to imitate this Japanese style? If so, use black, red, gold, or silver for your Mandala and then coat it with lacquer.

Cover decoration from a Japanese lacquered jewelry box ➤

179

Kingdom of Love

The eye, in which I see God, is the same eye in which God sees me. My eye and God's eye—this is one eye and one vision and one realization and one love.

Meister Eckhart, Dominican mystic (1260–1328)

The most well-known Christian symbol for the divine Trinity is the triangle. It is often shaped as an eye, which sees everything. But this is not meant as controlled overseeing, but rather an encompassing "royal" perception of objects. Such a sight is not a godly monopoly, but rather a goal that many mystics in both the West and the East have actually reached. The Apostle Paul found a beautiful image for that: he wished all seekers for God "illuminated eyes of the heart." He meant by this a loving recognition of reality, which leads to profundity. Who thus opens the "eye of the eye" with the heart, is characterized as warm-hearted, clear-sighted and with a deep closeness to everything.

The residence of the Holy Trinity, the "Kingdom of Love" (Jakob Boehme)
Germany (17th century) ➤

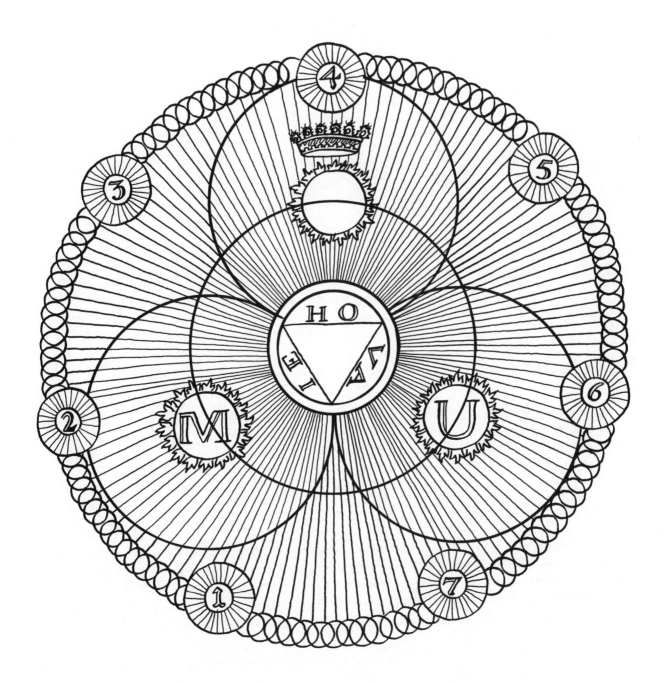

Hindu Lotus

The highest man uses his heart as a mirror. He does not investigate the objects and does not approach them; he reflects them, but does not hold on to them. Thus he can overcome the world and not be wounded. He is not the slave of his glory; he does not make any plans; he does not give himself to business; he is not the lord of knowledge. He pays attention to the smallest things and is yet inexhaustible and stays beyond the I. To the last he accepts what heaven gives, and yet has, just as he had, nothing. He remains humble.

Chuang-tze, philosopher (4th century B.C.E.)

At the birth of Prince Siddhartha, a lotus blossom opened, and the later Buddha strode into its middle, in order to see the eight directions of the horizon. In addition, he looked into the heights and the depths. Thus he obtained a complete spiritual orientation of the world, in which thought, feeling, intuition, and empathy are integrated.

We can comprehend this symbolic gesture of an ordered vision with this Mandala.

Lotus blossom, basalt ornament, India (7th century B.C.E.) ➤

Scottish Cross

Deep peace, a soft white dove to you
Deep peace, a quiet rain to you
Deep peace, an ebbing wave to you
Deep peace, red wind of the east from you
Deep peace, gray wind of the west to you
Deep peace, dark wind of the north from you
Deep peace, blue wind of the south to you
Deep peace, pure red of the flame to you
Deep peace, pure white of the moon to you
Deep peace, pure green of the grass to you
Deep peace, pure brown of the earth to you
Deep peace, pure gray of the dew to you
Deep peace, pure blue of the sky to you
Deep peace of the Flock of Stars to you.
In the name of the Three who are One,
And by the will of the King of the Elements,
Peace! Peace!

Fiona Macleod, "Invocation of Peace" (abridged, 1855–1905)

The labyrinthine network in the square center of the Scottish cross is presumably a sun rhombus, which represents Christ. The rising and setting of the sun were mythical images, to record life and death. For the Celts, the ancient sun symbol and the new symbol of Christ had become one. The round spirals on the outside, and also the inner square whorls show, alternately, a leftward rotation (death path) and a rightward rotation (life path). The cross unites both experiences and thus leads to a reconciling, peaceful look at the whole.

Centerpiece of a Celtic stone cross on the island of Inchbrayoe, Scotland ➤

Beginning and End

He is the happiest man,
who can set the end of his life
in combination with the beginning.

Johann Wolfgang von Goethe, author (1749–1832)

The age-old question about the relationship between the beginning and the end is the inner theme of this ornament, and there is an answer: endlessness. Life is an unending, intricate thread, and our own individual life is a part of it—that has, at the same time, a share in the whole. You will notice when coloring and entering into the shape that there are two ribbons interwoven with each other. Thus our own existence is always combined with others as well, with our ancestors and descendants, with our thoughts and actions. At the same time, the ribbons enclose two rings, archetypes for the outer and inner world. Everything is inseparably entwined within everything else. From all of this arises an artful unity which can be experienced, the secret and goal of all Mandalas.

Mandala from an ornament in St. Sebald, Nuremberg, Germany (Middle Ages) ➤

Mandalas according to Motifs

Mandalas according to Epochs and Cultures